Home Wine-Making

Also by H. E. Bravery

SUCCESSFUL MODERN WINE-MAKING

*H. E. Bravery*

# Home Wine-Making

MAYFLOWER
**GRANADA PUBLISHING**
London Toronto Sydney New York

Published by Granada Publishing Limited
in Mayflower Books 1969
Reprinted 1972, 1978

ISBN 0 583 19662 4

First published in Great Britain by
Arco Publications 1968


Granada Publishing Limited
Frogmore, St Albans, Herts AL2 2NF
and
3 Upper James Street, London W1R 4BP
1221 Avenue of the Americas, New York, NY10020, USA
117 York Street, Sydney, NSW 2000, Australia
100 Skyway Avenue, Toronto, Ontario, Canada M9W 3A6
Trio City, Coventry Street, Johannesburg 2001, South Africa
CML Centre, Queen & Wyndham, Auckland 1, New Zealand

Made and printed in Great Britain by
C. Nicholls & Company Ltd
The Philips Park Press, Manchester
Set in Linotype Times

# Contents

# FOREWORD

Let me begin by saying that it is quite easy to make any type or variety of wine, whether you like them light, medium or heavy, or dry, medium or sweet. It is also quite easy to produce excellent imitations of many well-known commercial products.

This may lead the uninitiated into thinking that to be able to do this means spending a lot of money. So let me assure you that your initial outlay for the essential utensils to enable you to follow this fascinating and rewarding hobby need be no more than one pound – a third of the value of your first gallon of wine. Let me also say, and stress most strongly, that it is an undeniable and somewhat amazing fact that only ten short years ago countless thousands in this country alone were following the antiquated and unsuccessful methods handed on by our grandparents.

Today, we follow simple methods which not only ensure success but also ensure that our wines have all the qualities of top-class products; full flavours, good aroma and bouquet, high alcohol content (which may be varied if desired), and that all-important, brilliant clarity, so difficult to achieve when old methods are used.

The pioneers took to the United States, Australia, New Zealand and other countries the only methods they knew of. Now, the people of these countries are also following modern methods – methods, I am proud to say, which I have had a lot to do with, and some of which I have evolved myself. As for recipes, I have evolved hundreds, many of which have made prize-winning wines for their users.

Surely no more need be said to prove that wine-making today is a simple, straightforward process with the very best results assured.

*Introduction*

## THE PAST TEN YEARS

This is not the place for a history of wine-making – let someone with an abundance of time to spare compile that. These few notes are included to show you just how far wine-making in the home has progressed in the past ten years.

In 1957, I and a group of friends evolved recipes and methods that have become popular throughout the world and which are today accepted as the best methods to use. Up until this time, people were following methods and recipes handed on by our grandparents – the very methods and recipes that spelt failure more often than success. The utensils they used were often dangerous to such an extent that they would pass lead into the wine, causing lead poisoning. Other utensils gave toxic substances into wines. Indeed, any utensils capable of holding a few gallons of liquor were pressed into service regardless of what they were made of.

There were no books on the subject to enlighten people, and the collection of recipes on the market were disastrous on account of the methods in which they were followed.

That we had evolved foolproof methods and recipes delighted us, but we could not bring these to the notice of those who would at once see the great achievement we had made. Magazine and newspaper editors simply were not interested, probably because they remembered home-made wines as they used to be – cloudy concoctions, low in alcohol, with precious little flavour and practically nothing to commend them other than that they were capable of producing really gigantic hangovers. Publishers were not interested in the only book that would bring to the wine-makers of the world these foolproof methods and recipes.

Ten years ago there was one small wine-making circle, the "Andover Circle": there was one firm retailing wine-makers' requirements, but only as a side line. The hobby was riddled with old wives' tales and superstitions, and was near to being considered a form of witchcraft. Those who heard of modern methods merely became disbelievers, for they simply would not graduate from the old methods of a century ago. There are still many thousands of disbelievers today; perhaps this book will help to convert them.

Make no mistake about this; wine-makers of the world owe a great deal to that famous newspaper columnist, Noel Whitcomb of the *Sun*. It was he, when he was writing his popular "Saturday Page" in the *Daily Mirror*, who saw the potential of modern recipes, methods and ideas. And it was through his publicity that they became popular. It is safe to say that, without his interest, the vast majority of wine-makers would today be using the antiquated recipes and methods handed on by our grandparents, with the result that home wine-making would have died a slow but natural death on account of the poor quality of the wine produced.

But what do we see today! There are over two hundred wine-making circles throughout this country alone, with many others in Australia, New Zealand, Canada and the United States, including "The Bravery Wine Club" of America, with its headquarters in New Mexico. This club was formed by a Dr. Rustebakke, of Placitus, Sandoval County. These wine circles hold their own competitions, which are always interesting. Regional groups of circles are now in existence and these also organize their own wine competitions. Then there is the National Conference and Show of Amateur Winemakers, where two thousand or more bottles are exhibited.

Where one firm had previously supplied the requirements

of wine-makers there are now about fifty, not to mention the large number of chemists and herbalists joining in the rush to meet the ever-growing demands for utensils and special ingredients. You would think by this time the modern methods and recipes were known to everybody in every corner of the world. Not a bit of it; there must still be millions throughout the world, and tens of thousands in this country, who still are not acquainted with these methods and who suffer failures more often than not, owing to the methods and recipes they use. Perhaps this book will help to convert a few thousands of them to the modern foolproof method and recipe; let's hope so, for their sake.

*Chapter One*

# SIMPLICITY THE KEYNOTE

Simplicity has been the keynote of all my books on this subject, for I believe that the average person wants simple recipes and methods to work with. I have never disguised the fact that wine-making can be a highly technical process for those who want to make it so. Indeed, behind the simple recipes there lie highly scientific and chemical processes which beginners need know nothing about. Even the best experts use simple recipes and methods. The fact that they use a lot of scientific appartus is because they simply must know how everything works. Having learned this, they are able to pass on recipes and methods that no longer require to be tested with scientific and chemical apparatus.

In other words, simple recipes and methods are often the result of years of research, about which you need to know nothing at all. This happy situation enables beginners to use simple recipes with top-class results assured.

## UTENSILS

As already mentioned, the utensils to begin with need cost no more than £1, and these are merely a 9 l (2 gallon) polythene pail, two 4.5 l (1 gallon) glass cordial bottles or carboys, a good size polythene funnel, two fermentation locks, and less than 2m (6ft) of polythene tubing for siphoning clear wines off deposits. Anything in the way of saucepans needed will already be in the house.

As will be seen, the polythene pail is used for fermentation purposes. The 4.5 l (1gallon) jars are used to contain the wine after the required period of fermentation in the pail. This is clearly stated in the methods. The fermentation lock, which is fully described in later pages, is fitted when the wine is put into jars. It is used to prevent spoilage yeast and bacteria from reaching the wine, and it also increases, or is instrumental in increasing, the alcohol content of wines. The polythene tubing is used to siphon, and this is not needed until your first batch of wine is clear and ready for bottling. The funnel, especially if this has a perforated disc-fitting, will be invaluable when straining solids from fermenting wines. A piece of muslin resting on top of the perforated disc will ensure that solids are withheld. When to use all these things is clearly given in the recipes and methods, but the fermentation lock, being the most important item of wine-making equipment, is described under its own heading.

It is surprising how, when you have made your first two batches of wine, you become quite expert in handling these simple items.

### THE FERMENTATION LOCK

When to fit this is clearly stated in the methods which follow each recipe, and how to fit it is shown in the illustration. As mentioned, this is the most important piece of equipment.

Under the heading "Spoilage" are details of how wild yeasts and bacteria are lurking in the hope of settling on fermenting wine, and these are attracted by the smell. But when a fermentation lock is fitted there is no smell of fermenting wines to attract them, although they are still close at hand, ready and waiting to do their worst. The fermentation lock is a guarantee against their gaining access.

When fitted to a jar of wine and filled to the level shown with some sterilizing solution, the gas formed during fermentation escapes through the solution in the form of bubbles. The solution closes up behind the bubbles, thereby preventing the air – and the wild yeast and bacteria that it carries –

from gaining access. But because the fermentati
off the supply of oxygen from outside, the yeast,
have oxygen if it is to ferment properly, obtai
from the sugar in the wine. In doing this the yeast uses more sugar, and therefore makes more alcohol, than it would if it obtained its oxygen supply from outside. Besides all this, the fermentation lock prevents evaporation of alcohol, retains the aroma and bouquet, and is generally instrumental in helping to make the top-class wines we want. Readers who have never before heard of the fermentation lock and who have made wines, will now realize why they have not produced wines of a sufficiently good quality.

## FERMENTATION

It has been seen that, having prepared the fruits, we add yeast, for without yeast the fruit-juice and water mixture would never become wine. But it might ferment and become "some sort" of alcoholic mixture, because the wild yeast and bacteria in the air would eventually reach it and set up fermentation, although this would never result in wine as we know it. These points are covered under the heading "Spoilage", so let me deal with the fermentation we start ourselves by adding yeast.

When we add yeast to the prepared must – fruit-juice and water mixture – it almost immediately begins to reproduce itself, producing millions of new yeast cells. To do this it lives upon the sugar, and produces as a by-product the all-important alcohol we want. It also alters the flavours of the fruits, creates bouquet and aroma, and therefore turns the must into wine. It is important to understand that yeast can use no more than 0.25 kg of sugar in 1 l of must (2.5 lb in 1 gallon). With this simple fact in mind we are able to judge how much sugar to use to obtain a dry, medium or sweet wine. 0.25 kg of sugar in 1 l of must (2.5lb in 1 gallon) will produce 14 per cent alcohol by volume. This is the most you can expect to make but it is quite enough. Therefore, if we use 0.25 kg of sugar to 1 l of must (2.5 lb in 1 gallon), all the sugar will be fermented out, leaving a dry wine containing 14 per cent alcohol. Use 0.3 kg of sugar per litre (3 lb in 1 gallon) 0.05 kg (0.5 lb) will be left unfermented to sweeten the wine, so that you will have a medium-sweet wine of 14 per cent. Use 0.35 kg of sugar per litre (3.5 lb per gallon) and you will have a sweet wine of 14 per cent. But because most dry wines are better with an alcohol content of less than 14 per cent, experienced wine-makers usually use about 0.2 kg per litre (2 lb per gallon) of sugar, and so obtain a bone dry wine of about 11 per cent. Many commercial dry wines are as low in alcohol content as this and sometimes even lower.

The reason why yeast can use only 0.25 kg of sugar per litre (2.5 lb per gallon) is because this amount makes 14 per cent alcohol, and this percentage of alcohol kills the yeast so that it cannot make more. Thus, when this happens, the wine ceases to ferment, and no matter how often you hear that the longer you keep wine the stronger it becomes, just laugh it off. I say this because, if the yeast is dead, no more alcohol can be made. *But* keep wines, as you should, and they certainly do appear a good deal stronger than when put away.

## CLEARING

Wines will not become brilliantly clear until fermentation has ceased, because the agitation caused by fermentation keeps minute solids in suspension. But as soon as fermentation has ceased, the wine should begin to become brilliant. The heavier solids will settle as fermentation slows, leaving only the minute solids that produce haziness to settle later. But do not expect brilliant clarity to come in a week or two; it often does, but it often takes a good deal longer. Many people talk themselves into believing something is wrong when their wines do not become brilliant right away. If, after six months from the time that fermentation has ceased the wine is still not brilliant, then and only then should you resort to the use of clarifiers.

I can honestly say that I never use clarifiers, because modern methods make wines that clear without their use. Root wines are often the exception here, but even these, when made properly and given approximately six to nine months in obstinate cases, usually clear to brilliance without assistance.

### CLARIFIERS

There are numerous clarifiers on the market; in particular, there are two enzymes now readily obtainable. One of these destroys starch which is given into potato and some other root wines, and another destroys pectin which is contained in all fruits. But by using modern methods the pectin is not released into the must, and therefore will not present a clearing problem.

The starch in roots is invariably boiled into the must, but if we handle things properly the yeast will turn the starch into sugar and ferment it out, leaving a brilliant wine. So, when making root wines keep the added sugar to the minimum to start with, so that the yeast turns to the starch for its sugar. Do not worry about this process producing fusal oil: only when sugar is produced from starch in this fashion on a large scale can the fusal oil become dangerous. The tiny amount of starch which is turned into sugar produces only a tiny amount of fusal oil and this, contained as it is in one or more gallons of wine, dilutes to such an extent that its presence is best ignored. Nevertheless, there are rare occasions when we do get a clearing problem with root wines and if you do happen – by sheer bad luck – to meet up with it, I can recommend the proprietary brand of clarifier known as *Pectasin.* Small packets cost 2½p and contain

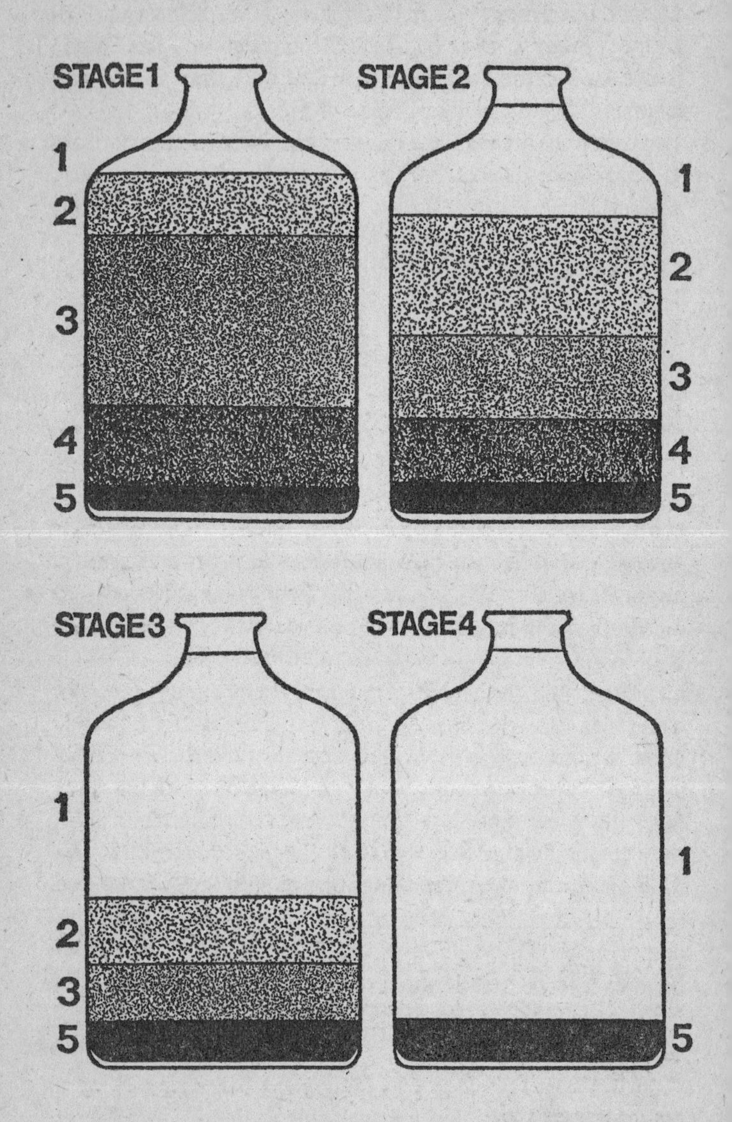
STAGE 1
1
2
3
4
5
STAGE 2
1
2
3
4
5
STAGE 3
1
2
3
5
STAGE 4
1
5

enough to clear 4.5 l (1 gallon) of wine. Merely take a little of the unclear wine and mix the Pectasin thoroughly into it, and then stir this into the wine itself. A better plan, if you happen to be transferring wine to a jar at this time, would be to put the treated sample into the new jar and to pour the bulk onto this clarifier. In this way you will get a better mixing.

### SPOILAGE

In the old days wines were spoiled more often than not; they turned insipid and flat, became bitter, very much over-acid, oily and unpalatable, acquired the smell of mouse-dung or turned into vinegar, and there are many other ways in which they were spoiled, and indeed *are* spoiled today, when old methods are used. While modern methods prevent all these calamities you should still know about them so that you understand the reason for making wines as we do today. You will then be able to appreciate the reason for using a fermentation lock and for using the easily made-up sterilising solution. Furthermore, you will be able to appreciate the simplicity of modern methods.

Wild yeasts and the bacteria that ruin wines are on the fruits we use, and boiling to destroy them, as in the old methods, caused pectin to get into the must so that wines never became clear. So, today, we destroy these spoilage yeasts and bacteria with Campden fruit preserving tablets, and details of how this is done are included in the recipes. It will be seen from this that those methods which advised

---

STAGE 1. 1 Brilliant wine. 2 Lightweight solids. 3 Mediumweight solids. 4 Heavyweight solids. 5 Sediment.

STAGE 2. 1 Brilliant wine. 2 Lightweight solids. 3 Mediumweight solids. 4 Heavyweight solids. 5 Sediment.

STAGE 3. 1 Brilliant wine. 2 Lightweight solids. 3 Mediumweight solids. 4–5 Heavyweight solids will have settled out now to become sediment; hence only four sections here.

STAGE 4. 1 Brilliant wine. 5 All types of solids will now have settled out to form sediment.

you to crush the fruits and let it ferment were merely allowing wines to be made with wild yeast and bacteria – which, as we have seen, cannot hope to make decent wine.

Wild yeasts and bacteria in the air are also on corks and inside bottles waiting to spoil the top-class wines we put into them. So we sterilize bottles and corks quite simply with a sterilizing solution, as described later on. If it were not for the fermentation lock and for covering the fermenting pail with sheet polythene, as described in the methods, airborne yeasts and bacteria would find their way into the vessels. Clearly then, the methods used today are designed to ensure success.

### STERILIZING

The act of sterilizing bottles and corks is the final step in ensuring that the wines we have made are not spoiled by wild yeasts and bacteria in the air which, of course, have settled inside bottles and on the corks. The simplest and surest means of doing this is to use a solution of sulphur dioxide made up as follows:

Obtain 57g (2 oz) of sodium metabisulphite from a chemist. This will cost about 5p. Put the powder into a polythene, china or glass jug and pour on about 0.6 l (1 pint) of warm water, stir this with a non-metal object until all the powder is dissolved. Then pour this into a 2.25 l (0.5 gallon) glass bottle (almost any chemist will let you have one for about 5p) and fill nearly full with cold water. Cork well and keep ready for use. On no account take a good sniff of this stuff with your nose near the bottles as the odour of sulphur can have the effect of causing some people to cough. Used in the normal process it will not do this.

When fermenting wine is put into a jar, the jar should be well rinsed inside with about 0.6 l (1 pint) of this solution and allowed to drain upside down for a few minutes before the wine is put into it. When bottling, put the corks to be used in a basin of this solution and put a saucer on top to ensure that corks are submerged. Then put about 150 ml (0.25 pint) of the solution into the first bottle to be used, shake it well so that all inside is wetted, and then pour into the next bottle and so on. Turn the bottles upside down to drain for a minute or two before use. The sterilizing solution may be returned to the bulk for re-use. The 2.25 l (0.5 gallon) made up as directed will retain its strength for ages.

Only sterilize bottles and corks at the time you propose to bottle wine – otherwise if they are left overnight, they will have to be done again. Before putting the sterilized corks into bottles, dry with a clean cloth. Plastic corks are now available quite cheaply and these need sterilizing in the same way. The advantage of these is they do not absorb wine and do not lose their shape.

## SIPHONING AND BOTTLING

There is no doubt that siphoning the wine into bottles is better than pouring from the jar, because if there is a deposit in the jar, this will be disturbed about half-way through the process. Siphoning is simplicity itself, but do not forget to sterilize the tubing. This can be boiled if you wish, or soaked in some of the solution. If you soak it, make sure the inside is treated. Home wine supply firms retail special siphons, but these are not necessary – though I will concede their usefulness. The tubing will do to start with.

Put the full jar of wine on a surface higher than the bottles. Put the tube in, about half-way down the jar, then suck the end at your fingers until the wine comes, pinch tightly, put the end in the first bottle and let the wine flow. When the bottle is nearly full, slow down the flow by gentle pinching, and stop the flow so that the wine reaches to about 6 mm (0.25 in) inside the neck of the bottle. Keeping hold of the tube, put it into the next bottle and let the wine flow again. As the level in the jar falls, lower the tube into it, but not so that the tube reaches the deposit, otherwise this will also be transferred into the bottle.

The best corks to use are, undoubtedly, the flat-topped, flanged or mushroom type. These used with the new plastic seals known as *Viskaps*, give your bottled wines the appearance of commercial products. Labels like those in the illustrations may be obtained cheaply from home wine supply firms – a list of them appears at the end of this book. A wide variety of labels are available, and all you need do is to write in neatly the details of the wines contained in the bottles. Do this before putting the labels on the bottles.

## STORING

The fact that nobody seems able to keep their home made wines long enough for storage problems to arise would seem to be evidence that they must be pretty good wines. Nevertheless, we all keep a few litres or gallons handy either in jars or bottles. Naturally, it is best to store wines in jars, not only because they improve in bulk, but also because they occupy less space in jars. Red and darker coloured wines should be put into stone jars, or if put into glass jars they should be kept in the dark. The same applies to wines in bottles, except that red and the darker coloured wines *must* be put into dark coloured bottles otherwise they may be adversely affected by light reaching them. Lighter coloured wines may be stored in glass jars or clear glass bottles and these always look a great deal better in punted bottles – that is, bottles with the bottom pushed up inside. The cupboard under the stairs is the spot chosen by most people as their cellar, and this seems to suit almost everybody without that blessing, the real cellar or semi-basement room.

## YEAST

As already mentioned, without added yeast our musts would not become wines. And upon the quality and type of yeasts depends the quality and, to some extent, the type of wine. Bakers' yeast was the only sort used until a few years ago, but today we have a wide range of very excellent wine yeasts to choose from. The cheapest and most convenient are those in dried form obtainable from home wine supply firms (see Appendix 1). A 2½p packet is enough for up to 23 l (5 gallons), and this is merely added in its dried form to the must as directed in the methods. Bakers' yeast will not make the best type of wine and on no account use yeast tablets intended for use as tonics.

If you have a batch of fermenting wine and are preparing a new batch, there will be no need to use fresh yeast. Merely stir up the fermenting batch and take about 150 ml (0.25 pint) into the new batch.

## YEAST NUTRIENTS

Yeast energizers, yeast foods and yeast nutrients are all the same thing, and these do play an important part in creating a good fermentation. Nutrients are merely blends of chemicals which are usually lacking in the musts prepared from materials other than grapes, and because the must ferments much better when these are present, we get a much better wine. Besides this, nutrients help to ensure that fermentation continues until the maximum alcohol level is reached and that the fermentation is more vigorous, as this means that the maximum alcohol level will be reached in a shorter time. Even so, fermentation will still take from three to four months in most cases. Use the nutrient according to the directions of the supplier and add this as directed in the methods. Most nutrients are merely added as a tablet or in powder form.

Warmth helps enormously in speeding fermentation, but on no account attempt to keep the wine over-warm. A temperature of about 18 to 21 °C (65 to 70 °F) is ideal, though fermenting wines will go along nicely in any part of the house during the warmer months. During winter, a cupboard near the fire or an airing cupboard over the hot-water tank will help a lot. If you use this, leave the door ajar so that the wine does not become overheated.

So there it is: a good yeast, a good nutrient and warmth during fermentation all play their part in producing good wines.

## TYPES OF WINE

It is important to understand that different fruits produce different types of wine, and that certain fruit makes several types of wine; for example, blackberries and elderberries make several different types of wine, while rhubarb will make only one sort. Rhubarb makes an appetizer wine and to try to make anything else from it will only lead to disappointment. It will be seen in the recipes how the different types of wines are achieved merely by altering the amount of fruit and sugar used, and you will save yourself disappointment by choosing carefully which type of wine you want to make before you begin. Having done that, the rest is relatively simple.

## SUGAR

Use ordinary, white household sugar. Invert sugar used by many wine-makers has certain virtues to commend it, but I have found that in the long run the extra expense is not worth the little difference it makes. Demerara and other brown sugars give their flavours into wines and often spoil the colour of certain wines; syrups and treacles do likewise.

Boiling the sugar with the water to be used serves two purposes: the sugar must be dissolved and we must not boil the fruit – so we boil the sugar in the water. Water, in any case, often contains wild yeast, so by boiling it we destroy the yeast which might otherwise set up undesirable ferments.

Honey, which is mainly invert sugar, is dealt with under the heading "Mead" – which is a type of wine on its own.

## TEA AND LEMONS

It will be seen that in root wine recipes and those for dried fruit, tea and lemons and sometimes oranges are used. The lemons add acid where this is lacking in the ingredients, and the oranges, besides adding a little acid, also add a little flavour where this is required. Acid is essential to a good fermentation and to a wine itself. Without acid, wines would lack bite and be quite lifeless. But be careful not to allow pips from the oranges or lemons into the must.

Tannin, which we obtain cheaply and conveniently by using tea, is also essential. Lack of tannin will often prevent wine clearing. The tea should be freshly made by using two teaspoonfuls of tea to 0.61 (1 pint) of water. This will be sufficient for 9 1 (2 gallons), so half that amount will be enough for one gallon. The tea should be strained before being added to the must.

## RIPE FRUITS ONLY

The use of fully-ripe fruits is far more important than most people would imagine. Under-ripe fruits contain a lot of acid, and it stands to reason that if this acid is put into the wine we get an over-acidic wine that makes us wince. Besides, under-ripe fruits do not make for the best wines, while fully-ripe fruits with good flavour and low acid content will make for top-class wines. And when I say ripe fruits only,

I mean every fruit that is used, whether it be elderberries, blackberries, plums or whatever you are using, for it needs only one or two under-ripe fruits to give an over-acidic bite to the wine.

### OLD ROOTS ARE BEST

There was an argument some time ago that potatoes added nothing to wine. If this were true, when you had finished making a gallon of potato wine, you would merely have potato water left. The truth is, that while potatoes cannot make wine in the real sense of the word and in relation to wines made from grapes, they do make a very good wine that is noted for its unexpected "kick". Old roots, potatoes, parsnips, carrots and beetroots are best. Those that have been stored through winter and made into wines during May or early June will give the best results. Potatoes left to shrivel slightly and sprout will give better results than any other, and do use the King Edward variety if you can. But don't use the sprouts. Parsnips, beetroots and carrots may be used younger, but it is best to use these when they are near the end of their season or have been stored through winter.

*Chapter Two*

# FRUIT WINES

In order to avoid too much repetition of detail in the methods described in this chapter, I have not included in the methods which follow each group of recipes the instruction to crush fruit by hand each day and cover again at once. So do bear in mind that in all the methods detailed in this chapter, the fruits should be stirred and crushed by hand once a day during fermentation.

It will be seen that in some of the fruit recipes we use dried fruit, with less fresh fruit than is normally required for a top-class wine. The benefits of this are two-fold. Firstly, in certain areas, wild fruits are less easy to obtain. Secondly, using less fresh fruit means quicker processing. But the advantages do not end there, for we are able to make a wider variety of wines by doing this than by using one basic ingredient. This does not mean that when using blackberries or elderberries we do not get a true elderberry or blackberry wine: we do, but the use of dried fruit allows us to make a variety of types – and this is important.

Bear in mind that a person not liking elderberry or some other wine made with the one fruit, will be absolutely delighted with that wine when less fruit is used in conjunction with dried fruits. Many wines, in the view of certain people, are too strongly flavoured. Using less fruit to reduce the flavour would result in a "thin" and not very interesting product. By using dried fruits we reduce the strength of flavour of the strongly flavoured fruits and produce full-bodied, fully-flavoured, robust wines, really worth having.

My trials with this type of wine-making revolved round

the problem of finding the most suitable dried fruit to use with the basic fresh fruit, as I did not want to alter to any appreciable extent the all-important flavour of the basic, fresh fruit. However, I do this sometimes when I want to test my knowledgeable friends, who assert that they can tell almost at once by tasting which fruit or fruits made the wine. You would be surprised how often I catch them out. The recipes containing dried fruits have been thoroughly tested and have turned out some really first-class products. Less sugar is needed when dried fruit is used. This is because most dried fruits consist of roughly 50 per cent sugar. Therefore, for each 0.5 kg (1lb) of dried fruit used, the normal amount of sugar required for the various wine types – dry, medium and sweet – is reduced by 0.2 kg (0.5lb). You have no need to reduce the amount of sugar yourself, as all this has been taken care of in the recipe.

## ORANGE WINE

A popular wine this, but often spoiled by being made over-strong in flavour.

Use thin-skinned oranges, as the thick pith lining of the thicker skinned often gives rise to bitterness in the finished product, though I can honestly say that I have never experienced this myself.

Oranges are often treated with wax or other materials to prevent spread of damage during transit, and for this reason each should be dipped in near boiling water and dried before being cut up – use a rough dry cloth or towel for this.

This is not a wine to make bone dry unless you know in advance that you must have all wines bone dry. In which case use 0.9 kg (2lb) of sugar instead of the amounts given in the recipes.

*For sweet wine*

12 large or 16 small oranges, 1.6 kg (3.5 lb) sugar, tea as in method, all-purpose wine yeast, nutrient and approximately 4.5 l (1 gallon) water.

*For medium-sweet*

10 large or 14 small oranges, 1.4 kg (3 lb) sugar, tea as in method, all-purpose wine yeast, nutrient and approximately 4.5 l (1 gallon) water.

*Method for orange wines*

Boil half the sugar in 3.4 l (3 quarts) water for 2 min, and when cool pour into fermenting vessel containing cut up oranges and their peel. Add 150 ml (0.25 pint) freshly-made, strong tea, nutrient and yeast, and ferment in warm place, covered as advised, for 6–7 days, crushing well by hand each day. Strain out solids and wring out as dry as you can. Return strained wine to cleaned fermenting vessel, covered as before, and leave to ferment for further 4–5 days. Then transfer to a 4.5 l (1 gallon) jar, leaving as much deposit behind as you can.

Boil remaining sugar in a pint of water for 2 min and when cool add to jar. If this does not fill to where neck begins, fill to this level with cooled boiled water, Then fit fermentation lock and leave in warm place until all fermentation has ceased. When this has happened remove lock and bung, fit new bung as tightly as possible and put wine in a cool place to clear. When clear, put half in a 2.25 l (0.5 gallon) jar and bottle remainder.

This wine is inclined to be rough when young, but it mellows down in about a year and if kept for three or four years, assumes many of the characteristics of an orange liqueur.

## RHUBARB WINE

It is far better to make this wine for use as it is intended – as an appetizer or refresher wine. Removing the acid and add-one does not have true rhubarb wine at all when one has finished; the basic ingredient (rhubarb) has merely been used to make a quite different wine. Rhubarb makes an excellent wine of its type and there is absolutely no reason at all for making it otherwise. A lot of poppycock is talked about the oxalic acid contained in rhubarb not being good for people. In excess, it would not be good for you, but the amount in wine is really very small and you don't take all that much wine at one sitting. I don't think I can recall hearing of anyone being harmed by stewed rhubarb, in which the oxalic acid is far more concentrated.

As mentioned, this is an acid wine, and one not popular with those who do not like this type of wine. But for those who like acid wine similar to many from the continent that are popular over here, rhubarb wine is a very easily made and a cheap substitute. A very excellent wine when made dry.

1.8 kg (4 lb) rhubarb, 1.3 kg (3 lb) sugar (1.1 kg (2.5 lb) for dry wine), tea as in method, all-purpose wine yeast, nutrient and approximately 4.5 1 (1 gallon) of water.

The rhubarb should be as fresh as possible. Weigh after removing leaves but before cutting off stumps. Cut prepared rhubarb into 25 mm (1 in) chunks after wiping clean with a damp cloth. Make sure the sticks are thoroughly cleaned. Boil half the sugar in 3.41 (3 quarts) of water for 2 min and pour into fermenting vessel. Add the rhubarb and tea and then the yeast and nutrient. Ferment in warm place until rhubarb becomes soft. To help this, crush by hand each day. This will not crush easily for the first day or so, but after three or four days the rhubarb will break apart. When this has happened strain through fine muslin, and return strained wine to fermenting vessel to continue fermenting, covered as before, for four or five more days. After this, pour carefully into a 4.5 l (1 gallon) jar, leaving as much heavy deposit behind as you can. Boil remaining sugar in a pint of water for 2 min and when cool add to the rest. If this does not fill to where neck begins, fill to this level with cooled boiled water; fit fermentation lock and leave to ferment in warm place until all fermentation ceases. When this has happened remove lock and bung, fit a new bung as tightly as possible and put the wine away to clear.

This wine will improve with age, but not so markedly as others, therefore it may be taken while quite young – this applies especially when made dry.

## CHERRY WINE

Several wine types may be made from cherries: the three recipes given below make the different types and you may choose which wine to make and then follow the method which may be used for each of them.

*Recipe No. 1*

An excellent table wine which may be made sweet or dry, using black cherries.

2 kg (4.5 lb) black cherries, 1.5 kg (3.25 lb) sugar for sweet wine (1.1 kg (2.5 lb) for a dry one), all-purpose wine yeast, nutrient and approximately 4.5 l (1 gallon) of water.

*Recipe No. 2* (do not make this dry).

2.7 kg (6 lb) black cherries, 1.5 kg (3.25 lb) sugar, all-purpose wine yeast, nutrient and approximately 4.5 l (1 gallon) of water.

*Recipe No. 3* using white or red cherries. (Do not make this sweet.)

1.8 kg (4 lb) cherries, 1.1 kg (2.5 lb) sugar, all-purpose wine yeast, nutrient, tea as in method, and approximately 4.5 l (1 gallon) of water.

*Method for cherry wine recipes*

Wash cherries and remove stalks. Put them in fermenting vessel and crush as much as possible – but you will not be able to crush them thoroughly at this stage. Pour on 1.1 l (1 quart) of cooled boiled water. Crush one Campden fruit preserving tablet in about an egg-cupful of warm water and stir this into the mixture. Leave for 1 h. Meanwhile, boil half the sugar to be used in 2.3 l (2 quarts) water for 2 min and when cool pour onto the cherries, but give them a thorough stirring first. Add 150 ml freshly made tea if you are using the recipe calling for this. Then add yeast and nutrient. Cover as advised and ferment in warm place for 8–9 days, stirring each day. After this, strain out solids through fine muslin and wring out as dry as you can. Return strained wine to cleaned fermenting vessel and ferment, covered as before, for 4–5 more days. Then transfer to a 4.5 l (1 gallon) jar, leaving as much deposit behind as you can. Boil remaining sugar in 0.6 l (1 pint) of water for 2 min and when cool add to jar. If this does not fill to where neck begins, fill to this level with cooled boiled water, fit fermentation lock and leave to ferment until all fermentation ceases. When this has happened, remove lock and bung, fit new bung as tightly as possible and leave in cool place to clear. When clean put half in a 2.25 l (0.5 gallon) jar and bottle the rest.

Dry wines may be used quite young – at six months or even earlier. The sweet cherry wines may be used young, but they improve vastly if kept for a year or two.

## LOGANBERRY WINE

Two very excellent wine types may be made with loganberries. The two recipes set out separately may be made by the same method. The first recipe makes a medium-sweet wine a little heavier and more full-bodied than the second which, being dry, is suitable for table use.

*Recipe No. 1*

1.8 kg (4 lb) loganberries, 1.5 kg (3.25 lb) sugar, all-purpose wine yeast, nutrient and approximately 4.5 l (1gallon) of water.

*Recipe No. 2*

1.4 kg (3 lb) loganberries, 1.1 kg (2.5 lb) sugar, all-purpose wine yeast, nutrient and approximately 4.5 l (1 gallon) of water.

*Method for loganberry recipes*

*Do not used damaged fruits.* Hull fruits and put them into fermenting vessel. Pour on one quart of cooled boiled water and crush fruit well by hand. Crush and dissolve one Campden fruit preserving tablet in about an egg-cupful of warm water and stir this into the mixture. Boil half the sugar to be used in 2.3 l (2 quarts) water for 2 min and when cool stir into mixture. Add yeast and nutrient, and leave to ferment, covered as advised, for 8–10 days. After this, strain out solids through fine muslin and wring out as dry as possible. Return strained wine to cleaned fermenting vessel, and leave covered as before for 3–4 days. Then pour carefully into 4.5 l (1 gallon) jar leaving as much heavy deposit behind as you can. Boil remaining sugar in 0.6 l (1 pint) of water for 2 min and when cool add to jar. If this does not fill to where neck begins, fill to this level with cooled boiled water. Fit fermentation lock and leave in warm place until all fermentation has ceased. When this has happened, remove lock and bung and fit new bung as tightly as possible. Put wine in cool place to clear. When clear, put half in a 2.25 l (0.5 gallon) jar and bottle the rest.

The dry will improve a good deal if kept a year or two, but this one may be used quite young if you prefer. The heavier wine should be kept at least a year before use as it will not be at its best until then.

## REDCURRANT WINE

It is best to make this light and dry though it may be made medium-sweet, but it is not at its best as a sweet wine. The same amount of fruits may be used for either dry or medium wine – merely alter the amount of sugar accordingly.

1.4 (3 lb) redcurrants, 1 kg (2.25 lb) sugar for dry (1.2 kg (2.75) lb sugar for medium), all-purpose wine yeast, nutrient and approximately 4.5 1 (1 gallon) of water. *Do not use damaged fruit* and make sure all are ripe. Remove stalks and put fruits in fermenting vessel and crush by hand. Add 2.3 l (2 quarts) water boiled and cooled. Crush and dissolve one Campden fruit preserving tablet in about an egg-cupful of warm water and stir this into the mixture. Leave for an hour or so. Meanwhile, boil half the sugar to be used in 1.1 l (1 quart) of water for 2 min and allow to cool. Then give redcurrants a thorough stirring and pour in the cool sugar syrup. Add yeast and nutrient and only two tablespoonfuls of freshly made tea, and ferment, covered as directed, in a warm place for 8–9 days. Strain out solids through fine muslin, wring out tightly and put strained wine into cleaned fermenting vessel to ferment for 3–4 more days. After this, put wine into a 4.5 l (1 gallon) jar leaving as much heavy deposit behind as you can. Boil the rest of the sugar in 0.6 l (1 pint) of water for 2 min, and when cool add to the jar. If this does not fill to where the neck begins, fill to this level with cooled boiled water. Fit fermentation lock and leave in warm place until all fermentation ceases. When this has happened, remove lock and bung and fit new bung as tightly as possible before putting wine in cool place to clear. When clear, put half in a 2.25 l (0.5 gallon) jar and bottle the rest.

Both these wines may be used quite young, but both improve with age – especially the medium-sweet type.

## BLACKCURRANT WINE

A lot of people who ought to know better will tell you that you cannot make good wines with blackcurrants. The truth is that you can make some of the finest home-made wine with them, and it would pay anybody with a small garden to put in a few blackcurrant bushes.

Three wine types may be made with this fruit by the one method. To achieve this you need three different recipes.

*A sweet Burgundy style*

1.8 kg (4 lb) blackcurrants, 1.6 kg (3.5 lb) sugar, all-purpose wine yeast, nutrient and approximately 4.5 l (1 gallon) of water.

*A dry Burgundy style*

1.8 kg (4 lb) blackcurrants, 1.1 kg (2.5 lb) sugar, all-purpose wine yeast, nutrient and approximately 4.5 l (1 gallon) of water.

*A very dry claret style*

1.1 kg (2.5 lb) blackcurrants, 0.9 kg (2 lb) sugar, all-purpose wine yeast, nutrient and approximately 4.5 l (1 gallon) of water.

*Method for blackcurrant recipes*

Make sure all fruits are ripe and do not use damaged fruits. Remove stalks, put fruits in fermenting vessel and crush by hand. Pour on 2.3 l (2 quarts) of cooled boiled water. Crush and dissolve one Campden fruit preserving tablet in about an egg-cupful of warm water and stir this into mixture. Leave for an hour or so. Meanwhile, boil half the sugar to be used in 1.1l (1 quart) of water for 2 min and when cool pour into blackcurrants, after giving them a thorough stirring. Add yeast and nutrient and ferment, covered as directed, in a warm place for 7–8 days. Strain out solids and return strained wine to cleaned fermenting vessel to ferment for 3–4 more days. After this, pour carefully into a 4.5l (1 gallon) jar, leaving as much deposit behind as you can. Boil remaining sugar in 0.6l (1 pint) of water for 2 min and when cool add to rest. If this does not fill jar to where neck begins, fill to this level with cooled boiled water. Fit fermentation lock and leave until all fermentation ceases. When this has happened remove lock and bung and fit new bung as tightly as possible and put wine in cool place to clear. When clear, put half in a 2.25 l (0.5 gallon) jar and bottle the rest.

The claret style may be used within three months – though at this stage it may still be a little rough. At six months it should have lost its roughness. The other two will improve a good deal if kept. The sweet will improve and keep on improving for five years or more.

## ELDERBERRY WINE

The fact that almost every home wine-maker makes this wine should be sufficient proof that it really is good. Indeed, I have written elsewhere that elderberries are the poor man's grape. Recipes for this wine are legion; all are different yet all basically the same. But though the types of wine that can be made from this fruit are many, I have chosen three basic recipes which will suffice any wine-maker. Do not make the heavy port style unless you are prepared to wait three years before using it. This is because it will be rough, and perhaps sharp to the palate as well, until that age. After this it will mellow to become a really marvellous product worth keeping for two or three more years.

It is important that all fruits are ripe. Do not make dry wine with this fruit. It can be done successfully, but you need a good deal of experience. Do, please, ignore anybody who tells you to add a few cloves to this wine.

*A heavy port style*

2.3–2.7 kg (5–6 lb) elderberries, 1.6 kg (3.5 lb) sugar, all-purpose wine yeast, nutrient and approximately 4.5 1 (1 gallon) of water.

*A Burgundy style*

1.8 kg (4 lb) elderberries, 1.4 kg (3 lb) sugar, all-purpose wine yeast, nutrient and approximately 4.5 1 (1 gallon) of water.

*A delightful medium light wine*

1.4 kg (3 lb) elderberries, 1.4 kg (3 lb) sugar, all-purpose wine yeast, nutrient and approximately 4.5 1 (1 gallon) of water.

*Method for elderberry wines*

Strip berries from stalks (do not worry if you crush a few doing this) and put them in fermenting vessel. Crush well by hand and mix in 1.11 (1 quart) of cooled boiled water. Crush one Campden fruit preserving tablet in about an egg-cupful of water and stir this into mixture. Leave for an hour or so. Meanwhile, boil half the sugar to be used in 2.3 1 (2 quarts) of water for 2 min, and when cool stir this into the mixture after giving berries a thorough stirring. Add yeast and nutrient and ferment, covered as advised, in a warm place for 8–10 days (but only 6 days if the heavy port style is being made). After this, strain out solids and return strained wine to clean fermenting vessel to ferment for further 4–5 days. After this, pour carefully into a 4.5 l (1 gallon) jar, leaving as much deposit behind as you can. Boil remaining sugar in 0.6 l (1 pint) of water for 2 min, and when cool add to jar. If this does not fill to where neck begins, fill to this level with cooled boiled water. Fit fermentation lock and leave until all fermentation has ceased. When this has happened, remove lock and bung and fit new bung as tightly as possible. Put wine in cool place to clear. When clear, put half in a 2.25 l (0.5 gallon) jar and bottle the remainder.

As already mentioned, the heavy port style should not be made unless you are prepared to wait at least three years before using. The Burgundy style will be quite a good wine after one year of keeping, but will improve beyond recognition if kept for two or three years. The lighter wine will be quite drinkable after one year, but like the other two, it will improve vastly with keeping.

## BLACKBERRY WINE

Another of those easily obtainable wild fruits which make a variety of first-class wines. Cultivated blackberries may be used quite satisfactorily. The three recipes here make distinctly differing wine types.

*Burgundy style, sweet*

1.8 kg (4 lb) blackberries, 1.6 kg (3.5 lb) sugar, all-purpose wine yeast, nutrient and approximately 4.5 l (1 gallon) of water.

*Burgundy style, medium*

1.8 kg (4 lb) blackberries, 1.4 kg (3 lb) sugar, all-purpose wine yeast, nutrient and approximately 4.5 l (1 gallon) of water.

*An excellent imitation of Beaujolais*

1.4 kg (3 lb) blackberries, 0.9 kg (2 lb) sugar, all-purpose wine yeast, nutrient and approximately 4.5 l (1 gallon) of water. If 0.2 kg (0.5 lb) of elderberries is added to this, an even better imitation of Beaujolais will result.

*Method for blackberry wines*

Hull blackberries, put them in fermenting vessel and crush well by hand. If elderberries are being added, strip from stalks, add to blackberries and crush by hand.

Pour on 1.1 l (1 quart) of cooled boiled water. Crush and dissolve one Campden fruit preserving tablet in about an egg-cupful of water and stir this into mixture. Leave for an hour or so. Meanwhile, boil half the sugar to be used in 2.3 l (2 quarts) of water for 2 min and when cool stir into mixture after giving thorough stirring. Add yeast and nutrient and ferment, covered as advised, in warm place for 8 days.

Strain out solids through fine muslin and wring out tightly. Return strained wine to cleaned fermenting vessel to ferment for further 4 days.

Then pour carefully into a 4.5 l (1 gallon) jar, leaving as much deposit behind as you can. Boil the remaining sugar in 0.61 l (1 pint) of water for 2 min and when cool add to jar. If this does not fill jar to where neck begins, fill to this level with cooled boiled water, fit fermentation lock and leave in warm place until all fermentation ceases. When this has happened, remove lock and bung, fit new bung as tightly as possible and put wine in cool place to clear.

When clear, put half in a 2.25 l (0.5 gallon) jar and bottle the remainder.

The dry wine may be used at the tender age of six months and be an excellent wine – but this will improve a good deal if kept for one year. The other two should be a year old before they are used and will be even better at three years old.

## PLUM WINE

Made well with fully ripe fruits and kept a long time, plum wines develop into first-class products, making excellent light, dry and medium sweet wines as well as an excellent port-style wine. When using more than 2.7 kg (6 lb) of plums, two Campden tablets are necessary owing to the large amount of fruit being used. The three recipes below may all be used with the method that follows them.

*Light and dry*

1.8 kg (4 lb) plums, 1 kg (2.25 lb) sugar, all-purpose wine yeast, nutrient and approximately 4.5 l (1 gallon) of water.

*Less light and sweeter*

2.7 kg (6lb) plums, 1.4 kg (3 lb) sugar, all-purpose wine yeast, nutrient and approximately 4.5 l (1 gallon) of water.

*A heavier sweet wine*

3.6–4.5 kg (8–10 lb) plums, 1.6 kg (3.5 lb) sugar, all-purpose wine yeast, nutrient and approximately 4.5 l (1 gallon) of water. USE TWO CAMPDEN TABLETS IN THIS RECIPE.

*Method for plum wines*

Stalks and damaged fruits must not be included. Weigh plums without removing stones, and wash well if suspected to be slightly dirty. Put plums in fermenting vessel and pour on 2.3 l (2 quarts) of cooled boiled water (2.8 l (5 pints) if more than 2.7 kg (6 lb) of fruit is being used). Crush and dissolve one Campden fruit preserving tablet (two Campden tablets if more than 2.7 kg (6 lb) of fruit is being used) and dissolve powder in about an egg-cupful of water, and stir into mixture. Leave for about an hour.

Meanwhile, boil half the sugar to be used in 1.1 l (1 quart) of water (0.6 l (1 pint) if more than 2.7 kg (6 lb) of fruit is being used) and when cool, stir this into mixture after giving plums a thorough stirring.

Break up plums by hand, add yeast and nutrient and ferment, covered as directed, in warm place for 8–10 days. After this, strain out solids and return strained wine to fermenting vessel.

Boil remaining sugar in 0.6 l (1 pint) of water for 2 min and when cool add to remainder. Leave covered as before to ferment for 3–4 days. Then transfer to 4.5 l (1 gallon) jar, leaving as much deposit behind as you can. Fill to where neck begins, adding cooled boiled water if necessary (this may not be necessary with all recipes). Fit fermentation lock and leave in warm place until all fermentation has ceased.

When this has happened, remove lock and bung, fit new bung and put wine in cool place to clear. The heavier wine will take a bit longer to clear. When clear, put half in a 2.25 l (0.5 gallon) jar and bottle the rest.

All these wines improve vastly with age. The dry may be used at six to nine months, but the other two should be kept for at least a year.

## DAMSON WINE

Most disappointments with this fruit are due to their being used too soon. Late September is soon enough but they should be left on the trees as long as possible. The first October frost will not harm them.

This fruit does not make good dry wine, therefore we have the choice of two sorts – medium and sweet. The sweet is made with more fruit because it can be heavier than the medium sweet. Thus we are able to make two differing wines, but not merely different owing to the amount of sugar used.

*Medium heavy, medium-sweet*

2.7 kg (6 lb) damsons, 1.4 kg (3 lb) sugar, all-purpose wine yeast, nutrient and approximately 4.5 l (1 gallon) of water.

*Heavy, sweet*

3.6 kg (8 lb) damsons, 1.6 kg (3.5 lb) sugar, all-purpose wine yeast, nutrient and approximately 4.5 l (1 gallon) of water. USE TWO CAMPDEN TABLETS WHEN 3.6 KG (8 LB) OF FRUIT ARE USED.

*Method for damson wines*

Stalks and damaged fruits must not be used. Weigh fruits without removing stones, and wash well if suspected to be slightly dirty. Put fruits in fermenting vessel and crush well by hand. Pour on 2.3 l (2 quarts) of cooled boiled water. Crush and dissolve one Campden fruit preserving tablet (two tablets if 3.6 kg (8 lb) of fruit is used) in an egg-cupful of water and stir this into mixture. Leave for about an hour.

Meanwhile, boil half the sugar to be used in 1.1 l (1 quart) of water for 2 min and when cool add to the rest, after giving damsons a thorough stirring. Add yeast and nutrient and ferment, covered as directed, in a warm place for 8–10 days. Then strain out solids, and return strained wine to cleaned fermenting vessel. Boil remaining sugar in 0.6 l (1 pint) of water for 2 min and when cool add to mixture. Leave to ferment, covered as before, in warm place for further 4–5 days.

Then transfer to 4.5 l (1 gallon) jar leaving as much deposit behind as you can. Fill jar to where neck begins with cooled boiled water, fit fermentation lock and leave in warm place until all fermentation has ceased. When this has happened, remove lock and bung, fit new bung as tightly as possible and put wine in cool place to clear. Clearing will not be so rapid with this wine as with others, but it will become a beautiful, dark, tawny colour with a brilliance of its own if left to its own resources.

When clear, put half into 2.25 l (0.5 gallon) jar and bottle the remainder.

The medium may be used at one year old, but the heavier should be kept for two years at least – you will not regret this, I assure you.

## GOOSEBERRY WINE

A pale green table wine, slightly on the acid side and best made medium sweet: dry can be made from green gooseberries.

A distinctly different wine with a pale red colour can be obtained from a kilogram or two (a few pounds) of gooseberries left on the bushes to turn red. This one can be either medium, sweet or dry.

*Using green gooseberries*

1.4 kg (3 lb) gooseberries, 1.4 kg (3 lb) sugar, all-purpose wine yeast, nutrient and approximately 4.5 l (1 gallon) of water.

*Dry*

1.4 kg (3 lb) gooseberries, 1.1 kg (2.5 lb) sugar, all-purpose wine yeast, nutrient and approximately 4.5 l (1 gallon) of water.

*Using red-ripened gooseberries*

For dry use 0.9 kg (2 lb) sugar; for medium 1.1 kg (2.5 lb) sugar; for sweet use 1.4 kg (3 lb) sugar. Use less sugar in these recipes because fully ripe gooseberries contain more sugar and less acid than the green variety. 1.8 kg (4 lb) of red fruits are used for whichever type of wine is required.

*Method for gooseberry recipes*

Top and tail gooseberries, and on no account use damaged fruits or any affected by mildew. Put prepared fruits in fermenting vessel and pour on 2.3 l (2 quarts) of cooled boiled water. Crush and dissolve one Campden fruit preserving tablet in an egg-cupful of water and stir this into mixture. Leave for about an hour. Meanwhile, boil half the sugar to be used in 1.1 l (1 quart) of water for 2 min and when cool stir into mixture after giving gooseberries a thorough stirring. Add yeast and nutrient and ferment, covered as directed, in warm place for 7–8 days. Strain out solids through fine muslin, wring out tightly and return strained wine to cleaned fermenting vessel to ferment, covered as before, for further 3–4 days. After this, transfer to 4.5 l (1 gallon) jar, leaving as much deposit behind as you can. Boil remaining sugar in 0.6 l (1 pint) of water for 2 min and when cool add to jar. If this does not fill to where neck begins, fill to this level with cooled boiled water. Then fit fermentation lock and leave in warm place until all fermentation has ceased. When this has happened, remove lock and bung, fit new bung as tightly as possible and put wine in cool place to clear. When clear, put half into 2.25 l (0.5 gallon) jar and bottle remainder.

The dry wines made with either sort of fruit may be used at six months, but the others should be kept a year at least. Even the dry wine will improve if kept longer.

## CRAB-APPLE WINE

I have discovered – as many others doubtless have – that this wine is always best dry, with not too much flavour of the fruits, which should be well-ripened and free of blemishes. Being a dry wine, this is ideal for taking with meals.

2.3 kg (5 lb) crab apples, 1.1 kg (2.5 lb) sugar, all-purpose wine yeast, nutrient, tea as in method and approximately 4.5 l (1 gallon) of water. Quarter the fruits lengthwise avoiding cutting pips, and keeping as many pips out of the must as possible. Put cut up fruits in fermenting vessel and pour on 3.4 l (3 quarts) of cooled boiled water. Crush and dissolve one Campden fruit preserving tablet in about an egg-cupful of water and stir this into mixture. Leave for about an hour. Meanwhile, boil half the sugar to be used in 0.6 l (1 pint) of water for 2 min and when cool add to mixture. Add 150 ml (0.25 pint) freshly made tea, the yeast and nutrient, and ferment in a warm place, covered as directed, for 5 days.

Strain out solids through fine muslin and wring out as dry as you can. Put strained wine into cleaned fermenting vessel. Boil remaining sugar in 0.6 l (1 pint) of water for 2 min and when cool add this to the rest. Cover as before and leave to ferment for further 5–6 days. Then pour carefully into 4.5 l (1 gallon) jar leaving as much deposit behind as you can. If the jar is not filled to where neck begins, fill to this level with cooled boiled water. Fit fermentation lock and leave until all fermentation has ceased. When this has happened, remove lock and bung, fit new bung as tightly as possible and put wine in a cool place to clear. When clear, put half in a 2.25 l (0.5 gallon) jar and bottle remainder.

Being a dry wine, this may be used quite young – but if kept a year it loses a good deal of its roughness and a little of its natural astringency. The astringency and roughness of this wine when young has its appeal for a good many people – so try it young to start with.

## TOMATO WINE

This recipe comes from a Canadian reader who writes: "I have been making wines with your recipes for years now with unfailing success, and would like to send you this recipe for tomato wine. We here in Bancroft, Ontario, vouch for its reliability and send it to you with our best wishes."
1.8 kg (4 lb) ripe tomatoes cut up small, 0.1 kg (0.25 lb) chopped raisins, 1.6 kg (3.5 lb) sugar, 2 oranges, 2 lemons,

all-purpose wine yeast, nutrient and approximately 4.5 l (1 gallon) of water.

*Note.* The additions: "all-purpose wine yeast, nutrient and approximately 4.5 l (1 gallon) of water" are my directions, because this part of the writer's recipe is not applicable to England.

Put cut up tomatoes and raisins in fermenting vessel and pour on 4.5 l (1 gallon) of boiling water. Leave to stand for two days, stirring daily.

Strain through fine muslin, pressing out all juice without letting pips come through. Add sugar to strained juice and stir well. Then bring slowly to boil and turn off heat. When cool, add strained juice of lemons and oranges and then the yeast.

Ferment in usual way until fermentation slows down and then put into jar with fermentation lock fitted.

This is as far as my correspondent's directions go, but you will see from reading directions in other methods how to handle the wine hereafter. Merely treat it as you would any other fruit wine.

*Chapter Three*

# FRESH AND DRIED FRUIT WINES

## ORANGE AND RAISIN WINE

Please see notes regarding type of oranges to use, and for oranges treated with wax see the head of the orange wine recipe.

12 large or 16 small oranges, 0.5 kg (1 lb) raisins, 1.1 kg (2.5 lb) sugar, tea as in method, all-purpose wine yeast, nutrient and approximately 4.5 l (1 gallon) of water. Treat the oranges as advised in the orange wine recipe. Boil half the sugar in 3.4 l (3 quarts) of water for 2 min and pour into fermenting vessel containing the cut up raisins. When cool, add the cut up oranges and their peel. Add 150 ml (0.25 pint) freshly made strong tea, nutrient and yeast, and ferment in warm place for 7 days, crushing well by hand each day.

After this, strain out solids through fine muslin and wring out as dry as you can. Return strained wine to fermenting vessel and leave to ferment for a further 5–6 days. Then transfer to 4.5 l (1 gallon) jar, leaving as much deposit behind as you can.

Boil remaining sugar in 0.6 l (1 pint) of water for 2 min and when cool add to the jar. If this does not fill to where neck begins, fill to this level with cooled boiled water. Then fit a fermentation lock and leave in a warm place until all fermentation has ceased.

When this has happened, remove lock and bung, fit new bung as tightly as possible and put the wine in a cool place to clear. When clear, put half in a 2.25 l (0.5 gallon) jar and bottle the remainder.

This wine will improve vastly if kept for a year before using. After two or three years it takes on many of the characteristics of an orange liqueur. A wine to make in bulk for long keeping.

## RHUBARB AND SULTANA WINE

Please see notes regarding rhubarb and the type of wine it makes in the rhubarb wine recipe.

1.4 kg (3 lb) rhubarb, 0.5 kg (1 lb) sultanas, 1.1 kg (2.5 lb) sugar (0.9 kg (2 lb) for dry wine), tea as in method, all-purpose wine yeast, nutrient and approximately 4.5 l (1 gallon) of water. The rhubarb should be as fresh as possible. Weigh after removing leaves but before cutting off stumps.

Cut rhubarb into about 25 mm (1 in) long chunks after wiping clean with damp cloth. Make sure sticks are thoroughly cleaned.

Boil half the sugar in 3.4 l (3 quarts) of water for 2 min and pour over the cut up sultanas in fermenting vessel, then add the cut up rhubarb. Add 150 ml (0.25 pint) freshly made strong tea and when all is cool, add yeast and nutrient.

Cover as directed and ferment in warm place for 7–8 days, crushing by hand each day. After this, strain out solids squeezing as dry as you can. Return strained wine to cleaned fermenting vessel and continue fermenting, covered as before, for 4–5 more days.

After this, pour carefully into a 4.5 l (1 gallon) jar, leaving as much deposit behind as you can.

Boil remaining sugar in 3.4 l (3 quarts of water for 2 min and when cool add to the rest. If this does not fill to where the neck of the jar begins, fill to this level with cooled boiled water. Then fit a fermentation lock and leave in warm place until all fermentation has ceased.

When this has happened, remove lock and bung, fit new bung as tightly as possible and put in a cool place to clear.

When clear, put half in a 2.25 l (0.5 gallon) jar and bottle the remainder.

While this wine, like all others, improves with age, it does not develop into the rich, heavy sort as do most other fruit wines. For this reason it is a good wine to make for use while quite young.

## LOGANBERRY AND RAISIN WINE

Although loganberries alone produce a high quality wine, two very excellent wines may be made when this fruit is combined with raisins. The first recipe makes for a full-bodied, sweet wine; the second makes a lighter, medium-sweet sort.

*Full-bodied sweet*

1.4 kg (3 lb) loganberries, 0.5 kg (1 lb) raisins, 1.4 kg (3 lb) sugar, juice of one lemon, yeast, nutrient and approximately 4.5 l (1 gallon) of water.

*Light, medium-sweet*

1.1 kg (2.5 lb) loganberries, 0.5 kg (1 lb) raisins, 1.1 kg (2.5 lb) sugar, juice of one lemon, yeast, nutrient and approximately 4.5 l (1 gallon) of water.

*Method for loganberry and raisin recipes*

Hull fruit, put them in fermenting vessel with cut up raisins and pour on 1.1 l (1 quart) of cooled boiled water.

Crush and dissolve one Campden fruit preserving tablet in about an egg-cupful of warm water and stir this into mixture.

Boil half the sugar to be used in 2.3 l (2 quarts) of water for 2 min and when cool stir into the fruit. Add strained lemon juice, yeast and nutrient and leave, covered as directed, to ferment for 8–10 days. After this, strain out solids and wring out as dry as you can. Return strained wine to cleaned fermenting vessel and leave to ferment, covered as before, for 3–4 more days.

Then pour carefully into a 4.5 l (1 gallon) jar, leaving as much deposit behind as you can.

Boil remaining sugar in 0.6 l (1 pint) water for 2 min and when cool add to the jar. If this does not fill to where the neck of the jar begins, fill to this level with cooled boiled water. Then fit a fermentation lock and leave in a warm place until all fermentation has ceased.

After this, remove lock and bung and fit new bung as tightly as possible. Put wine in a cool place to clear. When clear, put half in a 2.25 l (0.5 gallon) jar and bottle the remainder.

Both these wines will improve a great deal with age.

## REDCURRANT AND RAISIN WINE

When using raisins with redcurrants we are able to make medium sweet or sweet wine. The amounts of fruit remain the same for both types, but the amount of sugar varies.

*Medium-sweet*

0.9 kg (2 lb) redcurrants, 0.5 kg (1 lb) raisins, 1 kg (2.25 lb) sugar, all-purpose wine yeast, nutrient and approximately 4.5 l (1 gallon) of water.

*Sweet*

0.9 kg (2 lb) redcurrants, 0.5 kg (1 lb) raisins, 1.2 kg (2.75 lb) wine yeast, nutrient and approximately 4.5 l (1 gallon) of water.

*Method for redcurrant and raisin wines*

Remove stalks from redcurrants and put them into fermenting vessel with cut up raisins. Add 1.1 l (1 quart) of cooled boiled water. Crush and dissolve one Campden fruit preserving tablet in about an egg-cupful of warm water and stir this into the fruit. Leave for about an hour. Meanwhile boil half the sugar to be used in 2.3 l (2 quarts) of water and when cool pour into fruit mixture. Give a thorough stirring and add two tablespoonfuls of freshly made strong tea. Add yeast and nutrient and ferment, covered as advised, in a warm place for 8–9 days, crushing by hand once a day. Strain out solids and press out as dry as you can, and put strained wine into 4.5 l (1 gallon) jar. Boil remaining sugar in 0.6 l (1 pint) of water for 2 min and when cool add to the rest. If this does not fill to where neck of jar begins, fill to this level with cooled boiled water. Then fit fermentation lock and leave until all fermentation has ceased. When this has happened, remove lock and bung and fit new bung as tightly as possible. Put wine in cool place to clear. When clear, put half in a 2.25 l (0.5 gallon) jar and bottle remainder.

Both these wines improve a great deal with age.

## BLACKCURRANT AND RAISIN WINE

When using raisins with blackcurrants it is best to aim at two wine types – medium sweet and sweet. This is not to say that you cannot make a dry wine while using raisins because you can; it is just that when making a dry wine using raisins and blackcurrants, there is a slight lack of the all-important blackcurrant flavour. But as this does not necessarily mean that you would dislike the wine, I will include a recipe for a dry wine as well, in case you would like to try it.

*Sweet*

1.4 kg (3 lb) blackcurrants, 0.5 kg (1 lb) raisins, 1.4 kg (3 lb) sugar, all-purpose wine yeast, nutrient and approximately 4.5 l (1 gallon) of water.

*Medium*

1.1 kg (2.5 lb) blackcurrants, 0.5 kg (1 lb) raisins, 1.1 kg (2.5 lb) sugar, all-purpose wine yeast, nutrient and approximately 4.5 l (1 gallon) of water.

*Dry*

1.1 kg (2.5 lb) blackcurrants, 0.5 kg (1 lb) raisins, 0.9 kg (2 lb) sugar, all-purpose wine yeast, nutrient and approximately 4.5 l (1 gallon) of water.

*Method for blackcurrant and raisin wines*

Remove stalks and put fruits in fermentation vessel with the cut up raisins. Pour on 1.1 l (1 quart) of cooled boiled water. Crush and dissolve one Campden fruit preserving tablet in about an egg-cupful of warm water and stir this into mixture. Leave for an hour or so.

Meanwhile, boil half the sugar to be used in 2.3 l (2 quarts) of water for 2 min and when cool stir into mixture. Give mixture a thorough stirring and let it settle down for a few minutes. Then add yeast and nutrient and ferment, covered as advised, in a warm place for 7–8 days.

Strain and wring out as dry as possible and return strained wine to cleaned fermenting vessel. Leave covered as before to ferment for further 3–4 days. Then pour carefully into 4.5 l (1 gallon) jar leaving as much deposit behind as you can.

Boil remaining sugar in 0.6 l (1 pint) of water for 2 min and when cool add to jar. If this does not fill to where neck begins, fill to this level with cooled boiled water. Then fit a fermentation lock and leave until all fermentation has ceased. When all fermentation has ceased, remove lock and bung, and fit new bung as tightly as possible. Put away to clear, and when brilliant, put half in a 2.25 l (0.5 gallon) jar and bottle the rest.

Keep the sweet and medium sweet for at least a year before using. If you have tried your hand at a dry wine while using raisins, this may be used at six months old. But even this one will improve a great deal if kept longer. The fact is that all these wines will improve for up to five years, and even over a longer period than this, on occasions.

### ELDERBERRY AND RAISIN WINE

The notes at the head of the elderberry recipe do not apply so strictly here because we are using less fresh fruits. However, I must repeat, do not make this wine dry, and on no account add cloves. I mention this because so many people advocate their addition. I think this must have originated in the days when failures were more frequent than successes; wily grannies used all sorts of spices to camouflage them – and the idea caught on that they were necessary. Nothing could be further from the truth. Indeed, add cloves and you will ruin what would otherwise be top-class products.

*Heavy port style, sweet*

1.4 kg (3 lb) elderberries, 0.5 kg (1 lb) raisins, 1.4 kg (3 lb) sugar, all-purpose wine yeast, nutrient and approximately 4.5 l (1 gallon) of water.

*Medium heavy, medium sweet*

1.1 kg (2.5 lb) elderberries, 0.5 kg (1 lb) raisins, 1.1 kg (2.5 lb) sugar, all-purpose wine yeast, nutrient and approximately 4.5 l (1 gallon) of water.

*Method for elderberry and raisin wines*

Strip berries from stalks and put them in fermenting vessel with the cut up raisins. Pour on 1.1 l (1 quart) of cooled boiled water.

Crush and dissolve one Campden fruit preserving tablet in about an egg-cupful of warm water and stir this into mixture.

Leave for an hour or so. Meanwhile, boil half the sugar to be used in 2.3 l (2 quarts) of water for 2 min and when cool add to the fruit. Give a thorough stirring and leave for a few minutes. Then add yeast and nutrient.

Cover as advised and leave to ferment in a warm place for 6–8 days. Strain, and press well, and return strained wine to cleaned fermenting vessel to ferment, covered as before, for 3–4 more days. After this, pour carefully into 4.5 l (1 gallon) jar, leaving as much deposit behind as you can.

Boil remaining sugar in 0.6 l (1 pint) of water for 2 min and when cool add to the jar. If this does not fill to where neck begins, fill to this level with cooled boiled water. Then fit fermentation lock and leave until all fermentation has ceased.

After this, remove lock and bung, and fit new bung tightly. Put wine in a cool place to clear. When clear, put half in a 2.25 l (0.5 gallon) jar and bottle remainder.

Both these wines may be used after one year, but do keep some for two years at least. Only those who keep them as long as this or longer will be able to appreciate how age improves these wines.

## BLACKBERRY AND RAISIN WINE

Wild or cultivated blackberries may be used with equal success, but if cultivated blackberries are used, add the juice of one lemon when putting fruit into fermentation vessel, or use a double handful of under-ripe fruits. When using raisins it is best to confine yourself to making two wine types – sweet and medium.

*Burgundy port style, sweet*

1.4 kg (3 lb) blackberries, 0.5 kg (1 lb) raisins, 1.4 kg (3 lb) sugar, all-purpose wine yeast, nutrient and approximately 4.5 l (1 gallon) of water.

*A lighter, medium Burgundy*

1.4 kg (3 lb) blackberries, 0.5 kg (1 lb) raisins, 1.1 kg (2.5 lb) sugar, all-purpose wine yeast, nutrient and approximately 4.5 l (1 gallon) of water.

*Method for blackberry and raisin wines*

Hull blackberries and put them in fermenting vessel, with lemon juice if being used. Crush well by hand and pour on 1.1 l (1 quart) of cooled boiled water. Add chopped raisins and mix well. Crush and dissolve one Campden fruit preserving tablet in about an egg-cupful of warm water and stir this into mixture. Leave for an hour or so. Meanwhile, boil half the sugar in 2.3 l (2 quarts) of water for 2 min and when cool stir this into the mixture, after giving fruits a thorough stirring. Add yeast and nutrient and cover as advised, and leave in a warm place to ferment for 8–9 days. After this, strain out solids and wring out tightly. Return strained wine to cleaned fermenting vessel to ferment for further 4–5 days, covered as before. Then pour carefully into 4.5 l (1 gallon) jar, leaving as much deposit behind as you can. Boil remaining sugar in 0.6 l (1 pint) of water for 2 min and when cool add to the rest. If this does not fill to where neck of jar begins, fill to this level with cooled boiled water. Then fit a fermentation lock and leave until all fermentation has ceased. When this has happened, remove lock and bung, fit new bung as tightly as possible and put wine in cool place to clear. When clear, put half in a 2.25 l (0.5 gallon) jar and bottle remainder.

These two wines often become tawny-coloured and develop a real headiness, but not until after a year or two in store. At three or four years old these are really remarkable wines.

## PLUM AND RAISIN WINES

I do not know the name of the variety, but if you can find those large black plums that attain the size of eggs, do by all means use these: otherwise Victorias or any other fully ripe plums. Keep these wines for two years or longer and nobody will believe you made them yourself, simply because they develop into first-class port-style wines with age.

Confine yourself to two wine types when using raisins, a heavy port style and a medium port style.

*Heavy port style, sweet*

2.7 kg (6 lb) plums, 0.5 kg (1 lb) raisins, 1.4 kg (3 lb) sugar, all-purpose wine yeast, nutrient and approximately 4.5 l (1 gallon) of water.

*Medium port style, less sweet*

1.8 kg (4 lb) plums, 0.5 kg (1 lb) raisins, 1.1 kg (2.5 lb) sugar, all-purpose wine yeast, nutrient and approximately 4.5 l (1 gallon) of water.

*Method for plum and raisin wines*

Remove stalks, and make sure all fruits are in good condition. Put plums in fermenting vessel with chopped raisins and pour on 2.3 l (2 quarts) of cooled boiled water. Crush and dissolve one Campden fruit preserving tablet in an egg-cupful of warm water and stir this into mixture. Leave for an hour or so. Then crush plums by hand and give mixture a thorough stirring. Boil half the sugar in 1.1 l (1 quart) of water for 2 min and when cool stir into fruit, giving another stirring. Add yeast and nutrient and ferment in warm place, covered as advised, for 8–10 days, crushing by hand each day. After this, strain out solids and wring out tightly. Return strained wine to cleaned fermenting vessel and leave covered as before to ferment for further 3–4 days. Then transfer to 4.5 l (1 gallon) jar, leaving as much deposit behind as you can. Boil remaining sugar in 0.6 l (1 pint) of water for 2 min and when cool add to rest. If this does not fill to where neck begins, fill to this level with cooled boiled water. Then fit fermentation lock and leave until all fermentation has ceased. When this has happened, remove lock and bung, fit new bung as tightly as possibe and put wine in cool place to clear. When clear, put half in a 2.25 l (0.5 gallon) jar and bottle the remainder.

*Note.* You may find the deposit rather heavier with these wines, and that after pouring into the jar the deposit which forms in the jar will be brownish in colour – this is nothing to worry about.

### DAMSON AND PRUNE WINE

This combination makes two excellent port-style wines, one heavy and sweet, the other lighter and sweet. To obtain the best results the damsons must be fully ripe.

*Heavy port style, sweet*

2.7 kg (6 lb) damsons, 0.5 kg (1 lb) prunes, 1.5 kg (1 lb) sugar, all-purpose wine yeast, nutrient and approximately 4.5 l (1 gallon) of water.

*A lighter, medium-sweet port style*

1.8 kg (4 lb) damsons, 0.5 kg (1 lb) prunes, 1.2 kg (2.75 lb) sugar, all-purpose wine yeast, nutrient and approximately 4.5 l (1 gallon) of water.

*Method for damson and prune wines*

Weigh both fruits without removing stones. Cut prunes down one side with sharp knife and put them in fermenting vessel with damsons. Crush well by hand and pour on 2.3 l (2 quarts) of cooled boiled water. Crush and dissolve one Campden fruit preserving tablet in about an egg-cupful of warm water and stir into mixture. Leave for an hour or so. Meanwhile, boil half the sugar in 1.1 l (1 quart) of water for 2 min and when cool pour onto fruit, after giving mixture a thorough stirring. Give another stirring after adding sugar and then add yeast and nutrient. Cover as advised and ferment in warm place for 8–10 days, crushing well by hand each day. Strain out solids and wring out as dry as you can. Return strained wine to cleaned fermenting vessel. Boil remaining sugar in about 0.6 l (1 pint) of water for 2 min and when cool, add to the rest. Leave to ferment, covered as before, for further 5–6 days. Then pour carefully into a 4.5 l (1 gallon) jar, leaving as much deposit behind as you can. If the jar is not filled to where neck begins, fill to this level with cooled boiled water. Then fit fermentation lock and leave until all fermentation has ceased. When this has happened, remove lock and bung and fit new bung as tightly as possible and then put in a cool place to clear. When clear, put half in a 2.25 l (0.5 gallon) jar and bottle remainder.

My exhortations to keep this wine – and others too for that matter – are usually only partially heeded. So let me again try to assure you that by keeping this wine for two years you will help yourself enormously in producing a top-class product. It is difficult for inexperienced wine-makers to know what quantity of wine to produce, so that some may be used and the remainder kept in storage. The best course is to make as much as you can, so that you can use some after a year and still leave yourself a sufficient amount to be kept until it is really worth having.

## GOOSEBERRY AND RAISIN WINES

Two quite distinctive wine types are to be had by combining green gooseberries with raisins, as this tends to lessen the acidity of the gooseberries – an important factor for those who do not like the sharper types of wines. No attempt should be made to make these into heavy wines. The best you can do in this respect is to make one medium and one light. Leave the making of the heavier wines to the ingredients best suited to this purpose.

*Medium – medium sweet*

1.4 kg (3 lb) gooseberries, 0.5 lb kg (1 lb) raisins, 1.1 kg (2.5 lb) sugar, all-purpose wine yeast, nutrient and approximately 4.5 l (1 gallon) of water.

*Light – medium dry*

1.1 kg (2.5 lb) gooseberries, 0.5 kg (1 lb) raisins, 1.4 kg (2.75 lb) sugar, all-purpose wine yeast, nutrient and approximately 4.5 l (1 gallon) of water.

*Method for gooseberry and raisin wines*

Put gooseberries in fermenting vessel and crush well by hand. Add chopped raisins and then add 1.1 l (1 quart) of cooled boiled water and mix well. Crush and dissolve one Campden fruit preserving tablet in about an egg-cupful of warm water and stir this into mixture. Leave for an hour or so. Meanwhile, boil half the sugar in 2.3 l (2 quarts) of water for 2 min and when cool add to fruits after giving them a thorough stirring. Add yeast and nutrient and ferment, covered as advised, and leave in warm place for 7–8 days, crushing by hand each day. Strain out solids, wring out as dry as you can and put strained wine into cleaned fermenting vessel. Cover again as before and leave to ferment for 3–4 more days. After this, pour carefully into 4.5 l (1 gallon) jar, leaving behind as much deposit as you can. Boil remaining sugar in 0.6 l (1 pint) of water for 2 min and when cool add to jar. If this does not fill to where neck begins, fill to this level with cooled boiled water. Then fit fermentation lock and leave in warm place until all fermentation has ceased. When this has happened, remove lock and bung, fit new bung as tightly as possible and put wine in a cool place to clear. When clear, put half in a 2.25 l (0.5 gallon) jar and bottle remainder.

This combination of fruits does not make for the heavy type of wines that must be kept for years before they develop to their true glory. This makes for the lighter wines that may be used at their best much younger than most others. But it will be to your advantage to keep these for at least a year before using.

## CRAB-APPLE AND RAISIN WINE

As mentioned in the crab-apple recipe, when using crab-apples alone it is best to make the wine dry. But those wanting a sweeter crab-apple wine may use raisins. The idea here is to lesson the strength of flavour of the fruit without lessening the quality of the wine. In making a sweet wine with crab-apples alone the effect of sweetness causes a dullness of flavour. But this is not the case when raisins are used. 2.3 kg (5 lb) crab-apples, 0.5 kg (1 lb) raisins, 1.4 kg (3 lb) sugar, all-purpose wine yeast, nutrient, tea as in method, and approximately 4.5 l (1 gallon) of water.

Quarter the fruit lengthwise, avoiding cutting pips if possible and removing as many pips as you can. Put cut up fruits in fermenting vessel with chopped raisins and pour on 3.4 l (3 quarts) of cooled boiled water. Crush and dissolve one Campden fruit preserving tablet in about an egg-cupful of warm water and stir this into mixture. Leave for about an hour. Meanwhile, boil half the sugar to be used in 0.6 l (1 pint) of water for 2 min and stir this into fruits, after giving a thorough stirring. Add 150 ml (0.25 pint) of strong tea, yeast and nutrient. Cover as advised and ferment in warm place for 5–6 days. Strain and wring out as dry as possible and return strained wine to cleaned fermenting vessel. Boil remaining sugar in 0.6 l (1 pint) of water for 2 min and when cool add to the rest. Leave covered as before to ferment in warm place for 10 days. Then pour carefully into 4.5 l (1 gallon) jar, leaving as much deposit behind as you can. If jar is not filled to where neck begins, fill to this level with cooled boiled water. Fit fermentation lock and leave in a warm place until all fermentation has ceased. When this has happened, remove lock and bung, fit new bung as tightly as possible and put wine in a cool place to clear. When clear, put half in a 2.25 l (0.5 gallon) jar and bottle remainder.

This wine is likely to be rough when young. It is best therefore to keep for at least a year before using. By this time it will have mellowed a good deal and will, if kept longer, develop into a first-class product.

### LOGANBERRY AND PRUNE WINE

Make one type of wine – a medium sweet – with loganberries and prune and you will have a wine to be proud of.

1.1 kg (2.5 lb) loganberries, 0.5 kg (1 lb) prunes, 1.4 kg (2.75 lb) sugar, tea as in method, all-purpose wine yeast, nutrient and approximately 4.5 l (1 gallon) of water.

Hull loganberries, cut prunes down one side with sharp knife and put both fruits in fermenting vessel. Pour on 1.1 l (1 quart) of cooled boiled water. Crush and dissolve one Campden fruit preserving tablet in about an egg-cupful of warm water, and stir this into mixture. Leave to stand for an hour or so. Meanwhile, boil half the sugar to be used in 2.3 l (2 quarts) of water for 2 min and when cool stir into fruits after giving them a thorough stirring. Add 150 ml (0.25 pint) of freshly made strong tea. Then add yeast and nutrient and ferment in warm place, covered as advised, for 8–10 days. After this, strain out solids, wring out as dry as possible and return strained wine to cleaned fermenting vessel. Boil remaining sugar in 0.6 l (1 pint) of water for 2 min and when cool add to rest, and leave to ferment for 3–4 more days. Then pour carefully into 4.5 l (1 gallon) jar, leaving as much deposit behind as you can. If the jar is not filled to where neck begins, fill to this level with cooled boiled water. Then fit fermentation lock and leave until all fermentation has ceased. When this has happened, remove lock and bung, fit new bung as tightly as possible and put wine in a cool place to clear. When clear, put half in a 2.25 l (0.5 gallon) jar and bottle remainder.

This wine, like all others, will improve a great deal with age.

## ELDERBERRY AND PRUNE WINES

This is another wine likely to become one of your favourites. With this combination we are able to make three types of wine, dry, medium and sweet, and all are top-class products of their type.

*For dry wine*

0.7 kg (1.5 lb) elderberries, 0.7 kg (1.5 lb) prunes, 0.8 kg (1.75 lb) sugar, all-purpose wine yeast, nutrient and approximately 4.5 l (1 gallon) of water.

*For medium wine*

0.9 kg (2 lb) elderberries, 0.5 kg (1 lb) prunes, 1.4 kg (2.75 lb) sugar, all-purpose wine yeast, nutrient and approximately 4.5 l (1 gallon) of water.

*For sweet (and heavy) wine*

1.1 kg (2.5 lb) elderberries, 0.7 kg (1.5 lb) prunes, 1.4 kg (3 lb) sugar, all-purpose wine yeast, nutrient and approximately 4.5 l (1 gallon) of water.

*Method for elderberry and prune wines*

Strip elderberries from stalks. Cut prunes down one side with a sharp knife. Put both fruits together in fermenting vessel and pour on 2.3 l (2 quarts) of cooled boiled water. Crush and dissolve one Campden fruit preserving tablet in an egg-cupful of warm water and stir this into mixture. Leave for an hour or so. Meanwhile, boil half the sugar to be used in 1.1 l (1 quart) of water for 2 min and when cool add to the mixture, after giving a thorough stirring. Add yeast and nutrient and ferment in warm place, covered as directed, for 6–7 days. Strain out solids and wring out as dry as you can. Return strained wine to fermenting vessel. Boil remaining sugar in 0.6 l (1 pint) of water for 2 min and when cool, add to the rest. Cover as before and ferment in warm place for further 5–6 days. Then transfer to 4.5 l (1 gallon jar), leaving as much deposit behind as you can. If the jar is not filled to where neck begins, fill to this level with cooled boiled water. Then fit a fermentation lock and leave until all fermentation has ceased. When this has happened remove lock and bung and fit new bung as tightly as possible. Put wine in cool place, and when clear put half in a 2.25 l (0.5 gallon) jar and bottle remainder.

The dry wine may be used quite young. The medium should be kept at least a year and will improve immensely if kept longer. The sweet really should be kept at least two years before using – but I know you may not be able to do this. However, do keep at least one bottle as long as this, just to prove to yourself that you should have kept it all for this length of time! These really do develop into quite exceptional wines.

### BLACKBERRY AND PRUNE WINE

Three more wine-types that will be acclaimed as something quite out of the ordinary. Make these dry, medium or sweet.

*For dry*

0.9 kg (2 lb) blackberries, 0.5 kg (1 lb) prunes, 0.9 kg (2 lb) sugar, all-purpose wine yeast, nutrient and approximately 4.5 l (1 gallon) of water.

*For medium*

0.9 kg (2 lb) blackberries, 0.7 kg (1.5 lb) prunes, 1.1 kg (2.5 lb) sugar, all-purpose wine yeast, nutrient and approximately 4.5 l (1 gallon) of water.

*For sweet*

1.4 kg (3 lb) blackberries, 0.5 kg (1 lb) prunes, 1.4 kg (3 lb) sugar, all-purpose wine yeast, nutrient and approximately 4.5 l (1 gallon) of water.

*Method for blackberry and prune wines*

Cut prunes down one side with sharp knife and put them in fermenting vessel with blackberries. Pour on 1.1 l (1 quart) of cooled boiled water and mix well. Crush and dissolve one Campden fruit preserving tablet in about an egg-cupful of warm water and stir this into mixture. Leave for about an hour. Meanwhile, boil half the sugar to be used in 2.3 l (2 quarts) of water for 2 min and when cool stir into mixture, after giving fruit a thorough stirring. Add yeast and nutrient and ferment in warm place, covered as advised, for 7–8 days. Strain out solids and wring out as dry as possible. Return strained wine to cleaned fermenting vessel. Boil remaining sugar in 0.6 l (1 pint) of water for 2 min and when cool add to the rest. Leave to ferment in warm place, covered as before, for further 5–6 days. Then transfer to 4.5 l (1 gallon) jar, leaving as much deposit behind as you can. If it is not filled to where neck begins, fill to this level with cooled boiled water. Then fit fermentation lock and leave until all fermentation has ceased. When this has happened, remove lock and bung, fit new bung as tightly as possible and put wine in cool place to clear. When clear, put half in a 2.25 l (0.5 gallon) jar and bottle remainder.

The dry may be used rather sooner than the other two, both of which should be kept for at least a year before use. The sweet will improve beyond all recognition if some is kept for three or four years. The medium will improve for three years' keeping.

## BLACKCURRANT AND PRUNE WINE

This combination makes two very excellent wine types that develop into first-class products when made medium or sweet. But I have found that when made dry, this wine simply does not come up to expectations. Make it dry if you

1. With these few utensils countless thousands turn out a wonderful variety of top class wines.

**2. Straining: stage 1.** Tie one cloth to the vessel. Lay a loose cloth over this and strain the must: you will not then have to untie the string and gather up the material containing the solids. This nearly always results in an accident.

3. Straining: stage 2. How simple it is with one cloth tied to the vessel, allowing a loose cloth containing solid to be lifted up without accident.

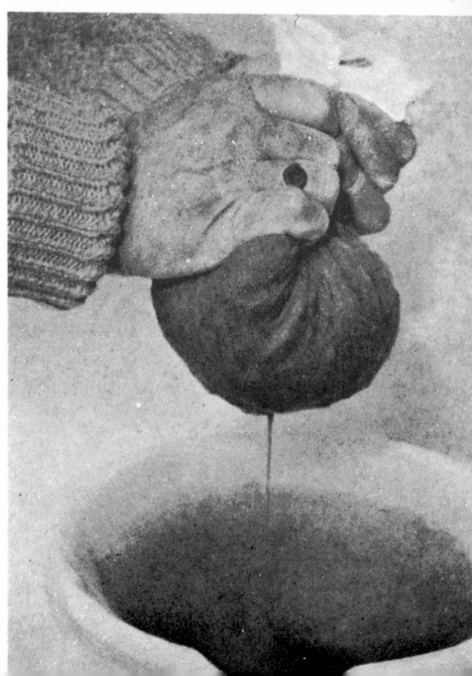

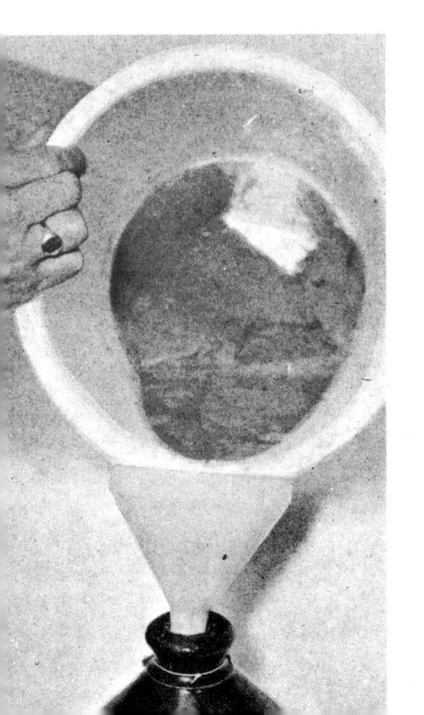

4 (*above*): Fermentation. During the vigorous fermentation stage the pips and skins form a cake on the surface of the wine. *Left*: 5. Leaving the deposit behind: I mention this often in the text—this is how it is done.

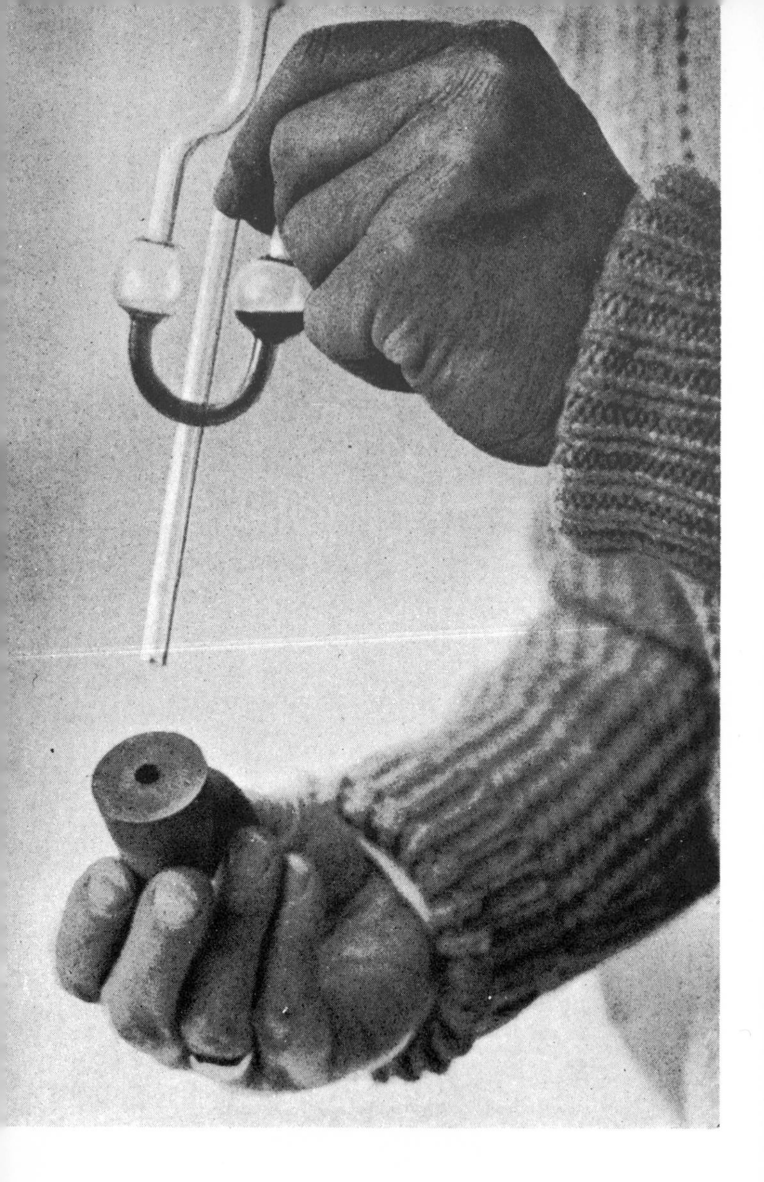

6. The fermentation lock with rubber bung. The lock will slide easily into the hole if the stem is wet. In all illustrations of the fermentation process, the sterilising fluid has been coloured for photographic purposes.

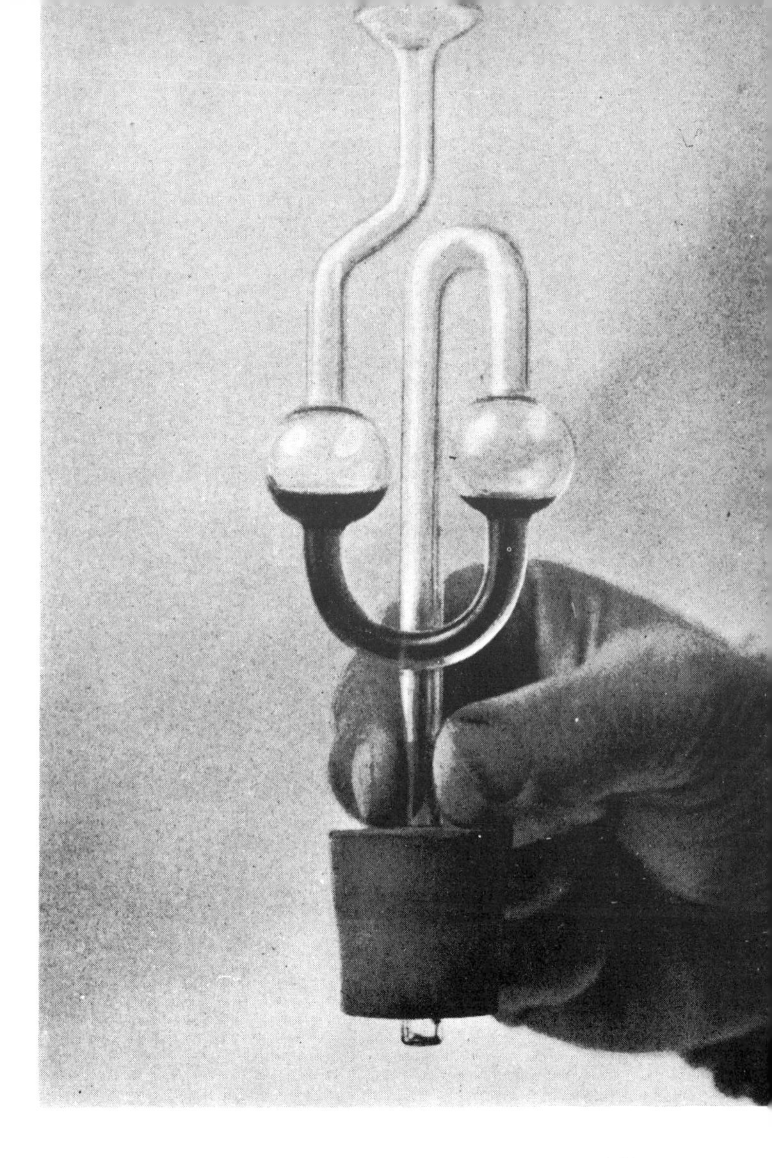

7. The fermentation lock: stage 2. Fitted to the bung and filled to the usual level.

8. The fermentation lock: stage 3. Pressing the unit into a jar of fermenting wine. Note how the fermentation bubbles, gathering at the shoulders of the jar. If the bung is wetted it will slip in easily.

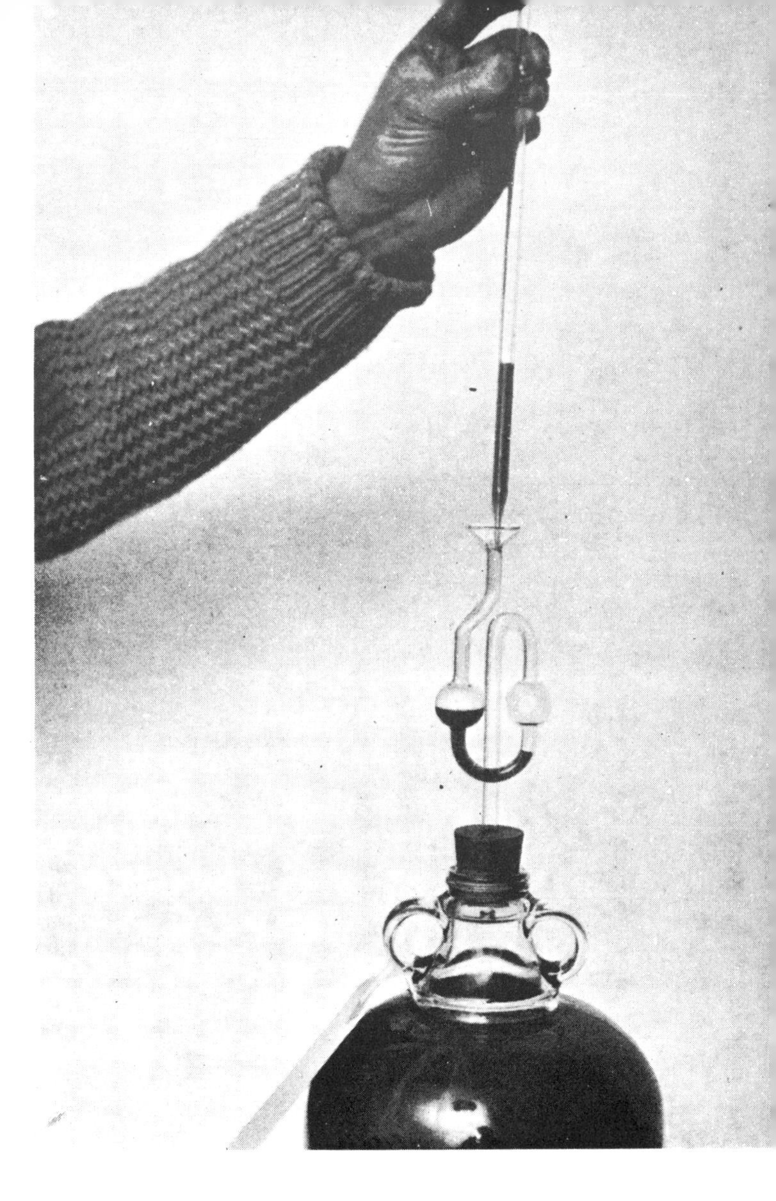

9. Topping up a fermentation lock.

10. The clearing process: stage
Wine, recently put into a jar, is still very cloudy with little deposit.

11. The clearing process: stage
Still very cloudy but with a hea
deposit built up.

12. The clearing process: stage 3. The wine is clearing slightly and is much paler in colour after one racking.

13. The clearing process: stage 4. The brilliant wine ready for siphoning into bottles. The clearing process has been illustrated in four pictures only; actually the process could have been shown in thirty or forty stages.

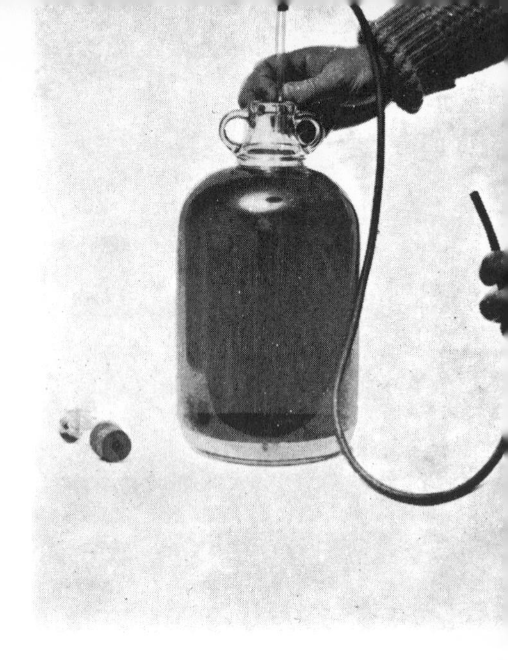

14. Siphoning: stage 1. The glass tube is lowered to the bottom of the jar, the upturned end remaining above the deposit.

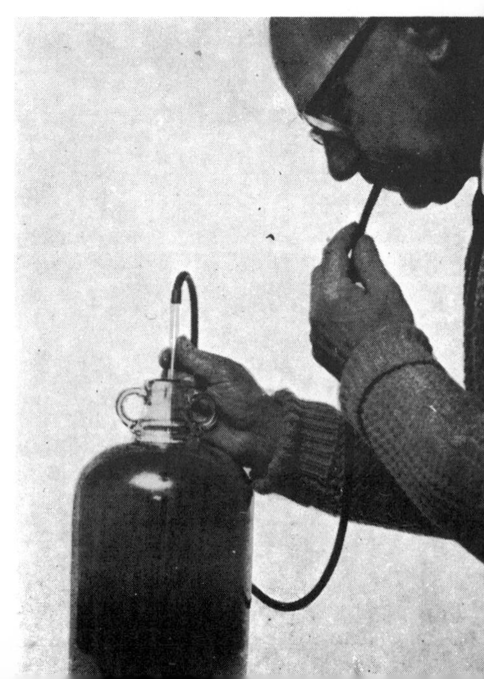

15. Siphoning: stage 2. Hold the glass tube gently but firmly to the neck of the jar. Suck the end of the rubber tube until the wine comes, then pinch tightly at your lips.

16. Siphoning: stage 3. Holding tightly to the tube, put the end into the first bottle and let the wine flow: when the bottle is full, pinch the tube tightly again and withdraw from the bottle. Repeat the operation until you have disposed of all your wine.

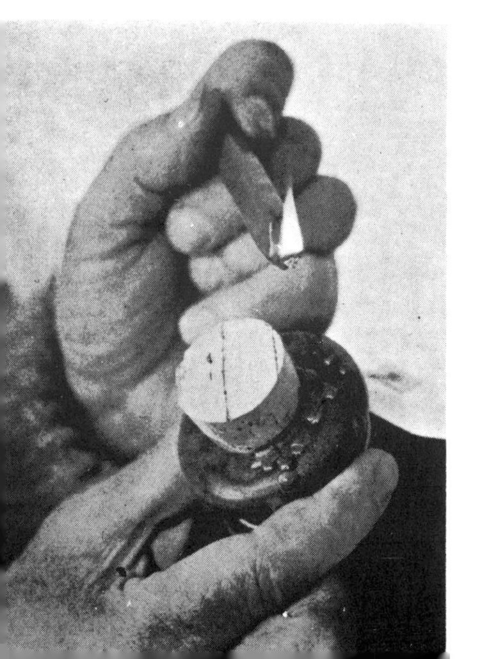

17. Sealing of the cork prior to storing.

18. Fitting capsules: stage 1. Merely open capsule by taking it between the finger and thumb; note the type of cork being used.

19. Fitting capsules: stage 2. Smooth down, pressing out the button that forms at the top.

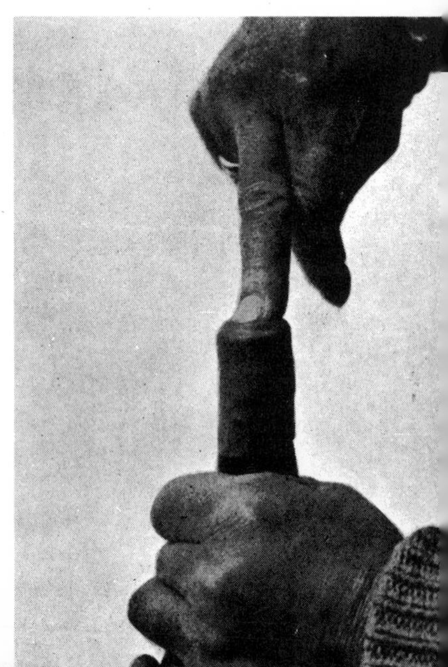

20. Fitting capsules: stage 3. The fitted capsule in its unshrunken state.

21. Fitting capsules: stage 4. Within a few hours the capsule will shrink to form a perfect airtight seal.

22. In the event of accidental re-fermentation while in storage, a polythene bag tied in place as shown will give ample protection.

23. The author's critical eye.

24. The final joy: labelling the finished product.

insist – by using 0.9 kg (2 lb) of sugar and the ingredients listed for the medium.

*Medium*

0.9 kg (2 lb) blackcurrants, 0.5 kg (1 lb) prunes, 1.1 kg (2.5 lb) sugar, all-purpose yeast, nutrient and approximately 4.5 l (1 gallon) of water.

*Sweet – and mildly heavy*

1.1 kg (2.5 lb) blackcurrants, 0.7 kg (1.5 lb) prunes, 1.4 kg (3 lb) sugar, all-purpose wine yeast, nutrient and approximately 4.5 l (1 gallon) of water.

*Method for blackcurrant and prune wines*

Cut prunes down one side with sharp knife and put them in fermenting vessel with blackcurrants previously crushed by hand. Pour on 1.1 l (1 quart) of cooled boiled water. Crush and dissolve one Campden fruit preserving tablet in about an egg-cupful of warm water and stir this into mixture. Leave for an hour or so. Meanwhile, boil half the sugar to be used in 2.3 l (2 quarts) of water for 2 min and when cool, give fruit a thorough stirring and then pour on the syrup-sugar water. Add yeast and nutrient and ferment in warm place, covered as advised, for 7–8 days. Strain out solids and wring out as dry as you can. Return strained wine to cleaned fermenting vessel. Boil remaining sugar in 0.6 l (1 pint) of water for 2 min and when cool add to the rest. Leave to ferment, covered as before, for 5–6 more days. Then transfer to 4.5 l (1 gallon) jar, leaving as much deposit behind as you can. If jar is not filled to where neck begins, fill to this level with cooled boiled water. Then fit fermentation lock and leave in warm place until all fermentation has ceased. When this happens, remove lock and bung, fit new bung as tightly as possible and put wine in a cool place to clear. When clear, put half in a 2.25 l (0.5 gallon) jar and bottle remainder.

If you make this dry, it may be used quite young. Many people must have all wines dry, so it will be a matter of taste as to whether you make it dry or not. Experienced wine-makers will know by judging from the combination of fruits whether they would like it dry or not. Inexperienced wine-makers will not have sufficient knowledge to guide them – hence my warning at the head of the recipe.

The medium should be kept for at least a year and will improve vastly if kept longer. The sweet, being a heavy type of wine, should be kept for at least two years to enable it to achieve its full glory.

## PEACH AND RAISIN WINES

Like apricots, peaches make a top-class product, but it is only in recent years that people have come to realise it. Three types of wine can be made in the certainty that they will please all tastes – provided you choose between dry, medium and sweet.

*For dry*

0.9 kg (2 lb) peaches, 0.5 kg (1 lb) raisins, 0.9 kg (2 lb) sugar, all-purpose wine yeast, nutrient and approximately 4.5 l (1 gallon) of water. Tea as in method.

*For medium*

1.4 kg (3 lb) peaches, 0.5 kg (1 lb) raisins, 1.1 kg (2.5 lb) sugar, all-purpose wine yeast, nutrient and approximately 4.5 l (1 gallon) of water. Tea as in method.

*For full-bodied sweet*

1.8 kg (4 lb) peaches, 0.9 kg (2 lb) raisins, 1.1 kg (2.5 lb) sugar, all-purpose wine yeast, nutrient and approximately 4.5 l (1 gallon) of water. Tea as in method.

*Method for peach and raisin wines*

Dip peaches in hot water to enable skins to be peeled off easily. Then cut up peaches, remove stones and put fruit in fermenting vessel with chopped raisins. Boil half the sugar to be used in 3.4 l (3 quarts) of water for 2 min and when cool pour over the fruits. Add 150 ml (0.25 pint) freshly made strong tea, yeast and nutrient, and ferment in warm place, covered as advised, for 7–8 days, stirring well each day. Strain and wring out as dry as you can and return strained wine to cleaned fermenting vessel. Boil remaining sugar in 0.6 l (1 pint) of water for 2 min and when cool add to the rest. Cover as before and leave to ferment in warm place for further 4–5 days. Then pour carefully into 4.5 l (1 gallon) jar, leaving as much deposit behind as you can. Fit fermentation lock and leave in warm place until all fermentation has ceased. When this has happened, remove lock and bung and fit new bung as tightly as possible. Then put wine in a cool place to clear. When clear, put half in a 2.25 l (0.5 gallon) jar and bottle remainder.

The dry may be used quite young and should be quite a good wine after six months. The medium needs a year to become really worth using and will improve for several years. The sweet, being both sweet and heavy, may be used after one year, but to be at its best it really needs to be left undisturbed for at least two years.

## APRICOT AND RAISIN WINES

This is another combination that makes for top-class wines, and, as with peaches, three types, dry, medium and sweet, may be made with confidence.

*For dry*

0.9 kg (2 lb) apricots, 0.5 kg (1 lb) raisins, 0.9 kg (2 lb) sugar, all-purpose wine yeast, nutrient, approximately 4.5 l (1 gallon) of water, and tea as in method.

*For medium*

1.4 kg (3 lb) apricots, 0.5 kg (1 lb) raisins, 1.1 kg (2.5 lb) sugar, all-purpose wine yeast, nutrient, approximately 4.5 l (1 gallon) of water, and tea as in method.

*For sweet*

1.6 kg (3.5 lb) apricots, 0.7 kg (1.5 lb) raisins, 1.4 kg (2.75 lb) sugar, all-purpose wine yeast, nutrient, approximately 4.5 l (1 gallon) of water, and tea as in method.

*Method for apricot and raisin wines*

Cut up apricots, chop raisins and put both in fermenting vessel. Boil half the sugar to be used in 3.4 l (3 quarts) of water for 2 min and pour while very hot over the fruits. Allow to cool to tepid and add 150 ml (0.25 pint) freshly made strong tea, yeast and nutrient. Cover as advised and leave in warm place to ferment for 7–8 days, stirring daily. Strain and wring out as dry as you can and return strained wine to cleaned fermenting vessel. Boil remaining sugar in 0.6 l (1 pint) of water for 2 min and when cool add to rest. If this does not fill to where neck of jar begins, fill to this level with cooled boiled water. Then fit fermentation lock and ferment in warm place until all fermentation has ceased. When this has happened, remove lock and bung, fit new bung as tightly as possible and put wine in a cool place to clear. When clear, put half in a 2.25 l (0.5 gallon) jar and bottle remainder.

The dry, like most dry wines, may be used quite young, say six months after clearing, and it does not improve as the others do when kept for a long time. The medium and sweet should be kept for at least a year undisturbed. The sweet will improve on keeping for several years.

*Chapter Four*

# FLOWER WINES

I have written elsewhere that flowers for wine-making are becoming a little less easy to find owing to constant building in country areas. Nevertheless, these wines, being what might well be called "country" wines, are still very popular, and there are enough flowers to enable enthusiastic beginners to make a few gallons each year for several more years at least.

Odd as it may sound, I have found it best to use honey for these wines instead of ordinary sugar. Experienced wine-makers will accuse me of confusing flavoured meads (*metheglins*) with true country wines, or vice versa. They can say what they like, for the fact is that I never cease trying to turn out something different, and experienced wine-makers must agree that my ideas have been the basis upon which modern methods and recipes are founded. True, you can use ordinary household sugar for these wines if you want to, but if you do this you will need to use slightly more flowers. For this reason, I have included recipes using honey with a certain amount of flowers and a recipe using sugar with more flowers.

All these wines are best made dry or medium dry to medium sweet. When made sweet, the sweetness seems to override the flavour of the flowers which, if the wines are to be at their best, must be delicate, as a pronounced flavour of flower is often quite distasteful.

*Quart (1.1 l) measure.* You may use a 1.1 l (1 quart) jug, and the petals are merely put into this and the jug bumped gently to settle them. On no account press them down by hand otherwise too many flowers will be used.

Elderflowers and hawthorn are merely pulled off the clusters. Gorse (mind the prickles) is treated likewise. With dandelions, when gathered close up the petals may be pulled off in one go, while the green part is held on the fingers. Rose petals may be collected as they fall or when they are about to fall. These may be gathered from day to day and made into wines when enough are available. But do not attempt to make rose petal wine unless you have plenty of rose trees or know someone who has, otherwise it may be too long between the first gathering and the last for the petals to remain in good condition. Three or four days is the longest that rose petals should be kept prior to making into wine.

Choose one of the recipes and then work to the simple method set out separately on Page 73. This method is quite suitable for all flower-wine recipes, whether honey or sugar is being used and whether the wine is being made dry or medium. The reason for arranging matters in this fashion is to avoid a great deal of confusion that could so easily arise when using two types of sugar, two different amounts of flowers, and while making two different wine types.

## DANDELION WINE

*Medium, using honey*

2.3 l (2 quarts) of petals, 1.7 kg (3.75 lb) honey, 150 ml (0.25 pint) freshly made strong tea, juice of 2 lemons, yeast, nutrient and approximately 4.5 l (1 gallon) of water.

*Dry, using honey*

2.3 l (2 quarts) of petals, 1.4 kg (3 lb) honey, 150 ml (0.25 pint) of freshly made strong tea, juice of 2 lemons, yeast, nutrient and approximately 4.5 l (1 gallon) of water.

*Medium, using sugar*

3.4 l (3 quarts) of petals, 1.4 kg (3 lb) sugar, 150 ml (0.25 pint) freshly made strong tea, juice of 2 lemons, yeast, nutrient and approximately 4.5 l (1 gallon) of water.

*Dry, using sugar*

3.4 l (3 quarts) of petals, 1.1 kg (2.5 lb) sugar, 150 ml (0.25 pint) freshly made strong tea, juice of 2 lemons, yeast, nutrient and approximately 4.5 l (1 gallon) of water.

## GORSE WINE

*Medium, using honey*

2.3 l (2 quarts) of gorse flowers, 1.7 kg (3.75 lb) honey, juice of 2 lemons, 150 ml (0.25 pint) freshly made strong tea, yeast, nutrient and approximately 4.5 l (1 gallon) of water.

*Dry, using honey*

2.3 l (2 quarts) of gorse flowers, 1.5 kg (3.25 lb) honey, juice of 2 lemons, 150 ml (0.25 pint) freshly made strong tea, yeast, nutrient and approximately 4.5 l (1 gallon) of water.

*Medium, using sugar*

3.4 l (3 quarts) of gorse flowers, 1.4 kg (3 lb) sugar, juice of 2 lemons, 150 ml (0.25 pint) freshly made strong tea, yeast, nutrient and approximately 4.5 l (1 gallon) of water.

*Dry, using sugar*

3.4 l (3 quarts) of gorse flowers, 1.1 kg (2.5 lb) sugar, juice of 2 lemons, 150 ml (0.25 pint) freshly made strong tea, yeast, nutrient and approximately 4.5 l (1 gallon) of water.

## ELDERFLOWER WINE

*Medium, using honey*

1.1 l (1 quart) of elderflowers, 1.7 kg (3.75 lb) honey, juice of 2 lemons and 2 oranges, 150 ml (0.25 pint) freshly made strong tea, yeast, nutrient and approximately 4.5 l (1 gallon) of water.

*Dry, using honey*

1.1 l (1 quart) of elderflowers, 1.4 kg (3 lb) honey, juice of 2 lemons and 2 oranges, 150 ml (0.25 pint) freshly made strong tea, yeast, nutrient and approximately 4.5 l (1 gallon) of water.

*Medium, using sugar*

1.7 l (3 pints) of elderflowers, 1.4 kg (3 lb) sugar, juice of 2 lemons and 2 oranges, 150 ml (0.25 pint) freshly made strong tea, yeast, nutrient and approximately 4.5 l (1 gallon) of water.

*Dry, using sugar*

1.7 l (3 pints) of elderflowers, 1.1 kg (2.5 lb) sugar, juice of 2 lemons and 2 oranges, 150 ml (0.25 pint) freshly made strong tea, yeast, nutrient and approximately 4.5 l (1 gallon) of water.

## ROSE PETAL WINE

*Medium, using honey*

4.6 l (4 quarts) of rose petals, 1.7 kg (3.75 lb) honey, juice of 2 lemons, 150 ml (0.25 pint) freshly made strong tea, yeast, nutrient and approximately 4.5 l (1 gallon) of water.

*Dry, using honey*

4.6 l (4 quarts) of rose petals, 1.4 kg (3 lb) honey, juice of 2 lemons, 150 ml (0.25 pint) of freshly made strong tea, yeast, nutrient and approximately 4.5 l (1 gallon) of water.

*Medium, using sugar*

5.7–6.8 l (5–6 quarts) of rose petals, 1.4 kg (3 lb) sugar, juice of 2 lemons, 150 ml (0.25 pint) freshly made strong tea, yeast, nutrient and approximately 4.5 l (1 gallon) of water.

*Dry, using sugar*

5.7–6.8 l (5–6 quarts) of rose petals, 1.1 kg (2.5 lb) sugar, juice of 2 lemons, 150 ml (0.25 pint) freshly made strong tea, yeast, nutrient and approximately 4.5 l (1 gallon) of water.

## HAWTHORN BLOSSOM WINE

*Medium, using honey*

1.1 l (1 quart) of hawthorn blossom, 1.7 kg (3.75 lb) honey, juice of 2 lemons, 150 ml (0.25 pint) freshly made strong tea, yeast, nutrient and approximately 4.5 l (1 gallon) of water.

*Dry, using honey*

1.1 l (1 quart) of hawthorn blossom, 1.4 kg (3 lb) honey, juice of 2 lemons, 150 ml (0.25 pint) freshly made strong tea, yeast, nutrient and approximately 4.5 l (1 gallon) of water.

*Medium, using sugar*

2.3 l (2 quarts) of hawthorn blossom, 1.4 kg (3 lb) sugar, juice of 2 lemons, 150 ml (0.25 pint) freshly made strong tea, yeast, nutrient and approximately 4.5 l (1 gallon) of water.

*Dry, using sugar*

2.3 l (2 quarts) of hawthorn blossom, 1.1 kg (2.5 lb) sugar, juice of 2 lemons, 150 ml (0.25 pint) freshly made strong tea, yeast, nutrient and approximately 4.5 l (1 gallon) of water.

*Method for flower wines*

Put the flowers in the fermenting vessel. Boil the sugar or honey in 4 l (7 pints) of water for 2 min, and while near-boiling pour over the flowers. Allow to cool, add strained lemon juice (and orange juice where this is being used), and stir in the strained tea. Add nutrient and yeast. Cover as directed and leave in warm place for 7–8 days to ferment. Stir daily and cover again at once. After 7–8 days, strain out petals and pour strained wine carefully into 4.5 l (1 gallon) jar, leaving as much deposit behind as you can. If the jar is not filled to where neck begins, fill to this level with cooled boiled water. Then fit a fermentation lock and leave until all fermentation has ceased. When this has happened, remove lock and bung, fit new bung as tightly as possible and put wine in cool place to clear. When clear, put half in 2.25 l (0.5 gallon) jar and bottle remainder.

Like other wines, flower wines improve with keeping. For this reason the medium types should be kept for at least a year before use. The dry wines, while improving a good deal, do not improve as considerably as the medium wines. Therefore, the dry flower wines may be used when six months old – though they will be better for having been kept a year.

*Chapter Five*

# ROOT WINES

Make no mistake about this, some really first-class products can be turned out from the common potato, carrot, etc. Experienced wine-makers make a wide variety of wines which they claim – with justification – cannot be matched. They are, in fact, of unique distinction.

*Special note.* It is a fact that wines made from starch-bearing ingredients, such as potatoes, rice, wheat and, in certain instances, apples, sometimes will not become crystal clear of their own accord. This is because starch has been boiled into the wine and nothing except a starch-destroying enzyme will shift it. However, in the methods used for these wines it will be seen that we use little sugar to start with. We do this not only because the yeast works better when little sugar is present, but also because, in starving the yeast of sugar in the early stages, we encourage it to convert the starch to sugar and ferment it out – thus leaving a wine free of starch cloud.

Many people have been puzzled in the past by the fact that on some occasions they could get a potato, or other wine made from starch-bearing materials, perfectly brilliant, while at other times they could not. Obviously, and quite unknown to them, they must have created conditions in which they starved the yeast of sugar at the outset. Enzymes are not, strictly speaking, for use by beginners. There is nothing complicated in using them, but it is far better to produce the brilliant wines in the normal way without having to use them. But, if you do happen to have a wine made from the materials mentioned that will not clear after six months of storage, it might be better to use a starch-destroying enzyme instead of waiting for it to become clear.

To clear 4.5 l (1 gallon) of wine, take 70 g (2.5 oz) of it and into this stir 14g (0.5 oz) of *Amylozyme* 100. This is obtainable from suppliers of wine-making equipment listed at the end of this book. The rest of the wine should be heated to 77°C (170°F) and held there for twenty minutes. It should then be allowed to cool to 38°C (100°F). When you have done this, stir in the enzyme. This may be added as it is, or strained into the wine through fine muslin. Having done this, keep the wine in a warm place and clearing should result in about an hour.

## CARROT WINE

A pale gold wine which, when kept for a year or two, develops into a top-class product.

1.4 kg (3 lb) carrots, 0.2 kg (0.5 lb) raisins, juice of 2 lemons and 2 oranges, 1.4 kg (3 lb) sugar, all-purpose wine yeast, nutrient, tea as in method, and approximately 4.5 l (1 gallon) of water.

*Method for carrot wine*

Scrub carrots thoroughly and remove blemishes. Grate them and boil gently for 15 min in 3.4 l (3 quarts) of water. Put half the sugar to be used together with raisins in fermenting vessel and strain onto them the boiling carrot water. Allow to drain for a few minutes and then discard carrots. Allow mixture to cool, and add the strained lemon and orange juice. Add yeast and nutrient and cover, as directed, to ferment in warm place for 10 days. After this, strain out raisins and squeeze well. Return strained wine to fermenting vessel and add 150 ml (0.25 pint) freshly made tea. Boil remaining sugar in 0.6 l (1 pint) of water for 2 min and when cool add to the rest. Cover again at once. Ferment, covered, in warm place for 6 days, and then transfer carefully to a 4.5 l (1 gallon) jar, leaving as much heavy deposit behind in the vessel as you can. If the jar is not filled to where neck begins, fill to this level with cooled boiled water. Then fit fermentation lock and leave in warm place until all fermentation ceases. When this has happened, remove lock and bung complete, fit a new bung pressing it in as hard as possible, and leave in a cool place to clear. When clear, put half in a 2.25 l (0.5 gallon) jar, bottle the remainder and do try to keep both for at least a year.

## POTATO WINE

Usually pale in colour compared with carrot wine and a first-class wine of its type. Best when medium sweet to medium-dry – not at its best when really dry.

0.9 kg (2 lb) potatoes, 0.5 kg (1 lb) raisins, 1.1 kg (2.5 lb) sugar, juice of 2 lemons and 2 oranges, tea as in method, all-purpose wine yeast, nutrient and approximately 4.5 l (1 gallon) of water.

*Method for potato wine*

Scrub potatoes thoroughly, removing eyes and blemishes. Grate them and boil gently in 3.4 l (3 quarts) of water until water becomes clear, but boil for not less than 15 min in any case. Put 0.2 kg (0.5 lb) sugar and the raisins in fermenting vessel and strain still-boiling potatoes onto them through fine muslin. Discard potatoes, allow mixture to cool and add strained juice of lemons and oranges. Add 150 ml (0.25 pint) freshly made strong tea, yeast and nutrient. Cover as directed and leave to ferment in warm place for 10–12 days. Strain out raisins and squeeze well. Return strained wine to fermenting vessel. Boil remaining sugar in 0.6 l (1 pint) of water for 2 min and when quite cool add to the rest. Leave to ferment in warm place, covered as before, for 5–6 days. Then pour carefully into 4.5 l (1 gallon) jar, leaving as much heavy deposit behind as you can. If the jar is not filled to where neck begins, fill to this level with cooled boiled water. Fit fermentation lock and leave in a warm place until fermentation ceases. After this, remove fermentation lock and bung complete, fit new bung pressing it in as far as possible, and put in a cool place to clear. When clear, put half in a 2.25 l (0.5 gallon) jar, bottle the rest, and do keep both for as long as you can before use.

## PARSNIP WINE

A white wine of considerable quality when kept for a long time. Best medium dry to medium sweet. Not a good wine to make bone dry or sweet.

1.1 kg (2.5 lb) parsnips, 0.5 kg (1 lb) sultanas, 1.1 kg (2.5 lb) sugar, juice of 2 lemons and 4 oranges, all-purpose wine yeast, nutrient, tea as in method and approximately 4.5 l (1 gallon) of water.

*Method for parsnip wine*

Peel parsnips and grate them. Boil gently for 15 min in 3.4 l (3 quarts) of water. Put sultanas and 0.2 kg (0.5 lb) sugar in fermenting vessel and strain onto them the still-boiling parsnips through fine muslin. Allow to drain for a minute or two and then discard parsnips. Allow mixture to cool, add 150 ml (0.25 pint) freshly made tea, yeast and nutrient. Strain in the juice of lemons and oranges, cover as directed and leave to ferment in warm place for 10 days. After 10 days, strain out sultanas and squeeze well. Return strained wine to fermenting vessel. Boil remaining sugar in 0.6 l (1 pint) of water for 2 min and when cool add to the rest. Cover as before and ferment for a further 5–6 days. Then pour carefully into a 4.5 l (1 gallon) jar, leaving as much heavy deposit behind as you can. Fill to where neck of jar begins with cooled boiled water, if this is necessary. Then fit a fermentation lock and leave in a warm place until all fermentation ceases. When this has happened, remove lock and bung. Fit a new bung, pressing it in as far as possible, and then put wine away to clear. When clear, put half into a 2.5 l (0.5 gallon) jar and bottle the rest. And do keep both as long as possible before using.

### BEETROOT WINE

Lovers of dry red wines are able to make a top-class product with garden beet. When made sweet, this wine lacks flavour, so make it only if you like dry wines.

When cooking beet for ordinary use the tops are merely twisted off and the beet cooked in their skins, but when making wines with them we must cut off the tops, as when preparing parsnips for cooking, and the beet must be peeled. If this is not done the wine might have an earthy flavour. Being a dry wine this may be used quite young.

1.4 kg (3 lb) beetroot, 1 kg (2.25 lb) sugar, juice of 3 lemons, tea as in method, all-purpose wine yeast, nutrient and approximately 4.5 l (1 gallon) of water.

*Method for beetroot wine*

Prepare beetroots as above and slice fairly finely. Bring to boil and simmer gently for 15 min in 3.4 l (3 quarts) of water. Strain boiling beets onto sugar in fermenting vessel and allow to drain for a few minutes before discarding the beet. Stir until sugar is dissolved, and when mixture is quite cool add the strained lemon juice. If there has been great loss through boiling, add 1.1 l (1 quart) of cooled boiled water. Then add the yeast and nutrient and ferment, covered as directed, in a warm place for 5–6 days. After this, pour carefully into a 4.5 l (1 gallon) jar, leaving as much heavy deposit behind as you can. If this does not fill jar to where neck begins, fill to this level with cooled boiled water; fit fermentation lock and leave in warm place until fermentation ceases. When this has happened, remove lock and bung. Fit a new bung as tightly as possible and put the wine away to clear. When clear, it may be bottled and used after a few months, but it develops into a better wine if kept for six months.

*Chapter Six*

# MEAD (HONEY WINE)

Mead-making is becoming very popular owing to the delightful results that can be obtained with readily available honey in tins. But although this honey makes good, general purpose mead, it cannot hope to compare with English honey – which makes the finest meads. There are many varieties of honey – gorse, clover and many more, including heather and others peculiar to the areas in which they are produced. And it has been the selection of the type of honey best suited to make the required type of mead that has resulted in meads of the very finest quality being produced.

When buying tinned honey – and it pays to buy bulk from one of the firms listed at the end of this book – you will have no choice but to accept that the honey is a blend of many varieties. Producers today are concerned mainly in producing honey for firms who retail it in bulk under a proprietary name; the result is that imported honey is sometimes blended with English honey, and many varieties are blended to give a uniform product, in the same way as wines are blended to make one wine of a popular sort. But even with our choice restricted to a few blended kinds we are able to make some really good meads.

Honey bought in tins is a sterile product, so there is no need to boil it, whereas English honey bought from an apiarist will have to be boiled or sterilized in some way.

My directions are for use with tinned honey. The cost of home-produced mead varies with the amount of honey purchased at one time. A 12.7 or 25.4 kg (28 or 56 lb) tin is the economical way to buy it, but a 3.2 kg (7 lb) tin for initial trials – just to see how things work out – will make 9 l (2 gallons) at a cost of about 10p per bottle. This compares favourably with the prices of commercial mead which vary between 42½p and 70p. The best way to work with a 3.2 kg (7 lb) tin is to make two separate batches of 4.5 l (1 gallon), using 1.8 kg (4 lb) for a sweet mead and 1.4 kg (3 lb) for a dry mead. In this way you will know quite soon which you prefer. If you do not like the dry mead you can sweeten it – it's as simple as that.

My notes about the need for acid and tannin in certain wines apply here because honey lacks both. The necessary acid and tannin are included in the basic recipe. But because honey contains about 70 per cent of sugar there will be no need to add sugar for fermentation purposes.

Assuming that you will start off with a 3.2 kg (7 lb) tin, the method is as follows:

*Sweet mead*

1.8 kg (4 lb) honey, juice of 2 lemons, 150 ml (0.25 pint) freshly made strong tea, yeast, nutrient and approximately 4.5 l (1 gallon) of water.

*Method*

If the honey is solidified, warm it gently and then mix it well with 3.9 l (7 pints) of boiled water that has cooled. Add lemon juice, tea, nutrient and ferment in polythene pail, covered as directed, in a warm place for 10–12 days. After this pour carefully into 4.5 l (1 gallon) jar, leaving as much deposit behind as you can. Fill to where neck begins with cooled boiled water, fit fermentation lock and leave until all fermentation has ceased. When this has happened, remove lock and bung, fit new bung as tightly as possible and put away to clear. When clear, put half in a 2.25 l (0.5 gallon) jar and bottle remainder.

Meads always improve with age, so do keep the half-gallon

jar for at least a year. The bottled mead may be used as required so that you are able to get a good idea of what that 2.25 l (0.5 gallon jar) will be like in a year or so. Being young, the bottled mead may be a bit rough – but not too rough to be enjoyed.

*Dry mead*

Use the remaining 1.4 kg (3 lb) from the 3.2 kg (7 lb) tin in exactly the same way as for sweet mead, using the same amount of tea, acid, tannin and water,

*Chapter Seven*

# THE USE OF SPECIAL FLAVOURINGS

There used to be a good deal of antiquated thinking about the use of flavourings for home-made wines. Most people – including myself – felt that they should be able to make the wines they want without resorting to the use of commercially produced flavourings, and, of course, they do. We make whichever type of wine suits us from whatever fruit we are using and we are all quite happy about it. So why bother with commercially produced flavourings?

The simple truth is this; although we are able to make the wine we want quite easily, the modern commercially produced flavourings give us a much wider range of flavourings to choose from. In other words, instead of being restricted to the few wine types and flavours we can achieve with wild and garden fruits and vegetables, we have a much greater choice.

A few years ago, people would not have dreamt of blending finished wines to achieve special results. But today, they blend, blend and blend simply because they have come to realise that this is the only means of obtaining certain types of wine which cannot be produced in any other way. All whiskies are a blend of several whiskies, and most commercial wines are also blended, while a very great number of them are flavoured with herbs. Were it not for this, vermouth, to mention only one, would not have come about.

In other books of mine I have detailed the use of *T'noirot* extracts. These give you wines flavoured as the well-known liqueurs – and what a success they are! But I *can* give you details of flavourings I have not hitherto mentioned: port,

Bordeaux, Burgundy, Madeira and sherry. However, using flavourings indiscriminately and without due consideration only leads to disappointment and waste of money. It may be elementary to warn you not to use port flavourings with potato wine, but you would be surprised how many might do this without realising that to create the right effect, port flavour must go with red wines. So when using flavourings we must use a suitable basic wine if we want to achieve a really first-class imitation. Having said that, I must concede that a lot of people who have been unlucky with certain wines make all sorts of interesting wines out of them with flavourings. To give just one example, a chap I know with a disappointing batch of parsnip wine (it was, incidentally, his own fault that it was disappointing), made a very excellent orange wine out of it with a flavouring. This is not to say that you can make orange wine as good as real orange wine with flavourings, but it does show what can be done. When using flavourings, please be careful not to overdo it, because it needs only a drop or so to flavour a lot of wine. The special dropper bottles in which these flavourings are sold will enable you to add them a drop at a time, and do sample for strength of flavour before adding too much. The sherry flavourings would go well with raisin wine because this already has the colour of sherry. But this flavouring could go with lighter coloured wines if you wish.

It is really a matter of common-sense application. Any of the home wine supply firms will let you have price lists (see Appendix), but at the time of writing I can say that a 12½p bottle will flavour more wine than you would want to flavour in one go – so the cost of an experiment in this connexion is not high.

*Chapter Eight*

# WINE-MAKING ON A LARGE SCALE

As mentioned at the beginning, the essential utensils to begin this hobby need cost no more than a pound, and, apart from a few additional jars at 12½p each, these utensils are all the average wine-maker needs to make 90–135 l (20–30 gallons) a year. Most amateurs make 9–13.5 l (2–3 gallons) a month, bottle so many litres each month, use so many litres each month and keep themselves busy and happy – or should I say "merry". For these people the utensils mentioned at the beginning will always be ample.

But for some people it is not always convenient to make several small quantities of wine each month. If three or four types of wine is all that a particular household requires, or when the operator does not have a great deal of time to give to the hobby, making wines on a larger scale is often important, particularly when consumption is likely to be heavy. This mention of heavy consumption used to amuse people years ago when home-made wines were not much good. Today, however, they hold their own with commercial products, and entertaining with home-made wines, taking them with meals and generally using them rather than buying from wine-merchants is becoming commonplace. So making wines on a larger scale, say, in three or four batches a year instead of a dozen, is often less bother and more economical, although the outlay for larger and more efficient utensils and apparatus is a bit higher. But this extra expense is well worthwhile when you have experience, and know in advance that what you are about to make will turn out to be precisely what you intended it to be – whether it be a good imitation of port, Beaujolais, Sauternes or whatever else it is. Many operators working on these lines and making four or five batches a year of, say, 35–70 l (8–15 gallons), invest in all sorts of useful gadgets and utensils, and claim that the expense more than pays for itself in time-saving alone.

Obviously, these people are not making it expensive just for the sake of it, and they look at it in the same way as a chap with a big garden who has little time to put into it: the motor-mower and electric hedge-clippers are investments that pay for themselves. So, in this chapter I deal with a few items which would be invaluable to those with experience who wish to make wines on a grand scale.

Naturally, making four or five large amounts four or five times a year involves a lot of work, but many experienced wine-makers prefer this to making twenty or so batches a year. Indeed, very many operators would have embarked upon this system long ago had they been aware of the utensils and apparatus available to them. But apart from convenience and time-saving, there is no doubt that wines made on a larger scale are very often better wines. They often keep longer and improve over longer periods than those made on a smaller scale. Besides, fermentation is frequently a good deal better, and the alcohol content consequently higher than it would normally be, and this alone would make for a higher quality wine.

However, be this as it may, you should not be influenced into the use of expensive apparatus unless you feel confident that it would be worth your while. A bit of a wit once wrote that 'making ten gallons is no more bother than making two, and the ten gallons last nearly twice as long.'

*Fermentation vessel.* For large-scale wine-making there is nothing to compare with the polythene dustbin, but if this is too big there are many smaller types of polythene vessels now available from home wine supply firms for making 35 or 45 l (8 or 10 gallons) at a time.

*Boiling the water.* Where water must be boiled, the ordinary wash boiler will be found quite suitable, provided it is not of galvanised metal.

*Jars.* Large stone jars can prove expensive, but distilled water bottles in their protective iron cradles can be had quite reasonably; 50p for a 22.5 l (5 gallon) and about £1 for a 45 l (10 gallon) size is not expensive. These used for the secondary ferment fitted with the ordinary fermentation lock are ideal. They are also ideal for the storage of even red wine, but if red wines are put into them the jars must be kept in the dark or painted outside with black paint, because light reaching red wines often spoils their colour. You could stand the jar on a large sheet of thick brown paper and then gather this up round the neck to keep out the light.

If large jars are used, the fermentation lock should be looked at from day to day to make sure the sterilizing solution has not become depleted. With the enormous amount of gas passing through there is a risk of the solution being expended in a short time – say, three or four days, and especially during the vigorous fermentation stage.

Barrels naturally have their advantages. If you use these make sure they are clean; sterilize them as for jars and do stand them on their beds. Those shaped blocks keep the staves off the floor and so prevent the weight from bending the staves. Bent staves cause leakage and expose wines to airborne diseases.

Any recipe in this book may be adapted to make any number of litres at a time. All you need do is multiply the amounts of ingredients by the number of litres you want to make. All my recipes are designed for 4.5 l (1 gallon) as this is the usual amount which inexperienced operators like to start by making. In this way they get the feel of things, can take stock of results, and generally decide which type of wine they want to make often and which type they do not want to make again. I know a chap who turns out 45 l (10 gallons) of elderberry "port", 22.5 l (5 gallons) of blackberry "claret" and 22.5 l (5 gallons) of carrot wine, amongst others, regularly each year. Experience tells him that these amounts of basic wines are those he will need, and while these are taking care of themselves he makes smaller quantities to find other sorts he likes. When he has discovered what he considers another "must", he makes this on a large scale as well. This is a good plan of operation, for it not only gives experience but it does allow for small experimental lots to be made while the larger batches are maturing. It also prevents one from making 45 l (10 gallons) of a wine that one may not, after all, be keen on. Not all tastes are the same, and it is important, when thinking of making a large batch, to know in advance that you like it.

Fruit presses, fruit juicers and other such utensils all play their part with individual operators, and there is a wide range to choose from. There is no need for me to include details of how these are operated because the suppliers issue instruction leaflets with their appliances. And whether you use one of these or not must depend entirely upon yourself – some operators do, others do not, and both seem to make wines as good as each other.

*Chapter Nine*

# MISCELLANEOUS RECIPES

Because these recipes are under this heading it should not be thought that they are merely an unimportant collection. The fact is, they make top-class wines of their kind, but because of their variety it is not possible to put them under specific headings of their own. A surprising number of people make wines with these recipes, ignoring wild and garden fruit, for the very simple reason that they like them. And, for myself, I cannot think of a better reason for making them. As I have gone to some pains to explain elsewhere, making the sort of wines you like is the whole basis of successful wine-making.

I can recall a conversation at a wine-making club where a friend of mine "put his foot in it" by openly declaring that he would not give tuppence for all the elderberry wine in the country. An almost shocked silence greeted this monstrous declaration. It was then that a lady tornadoed her way across the floor towards him demanding to know what was wrong with elderberry wine. "It's the finest home-made wine there is," she asserted. And then went on to describe its virtues.

My friend, being more diplomatic than I might have been myself, agreed with everything she said, but reminded her gently that not all people think the same way about the same thing. He then asked her what she thought of a particular commercial product becoming popular in this country today. "That stuff," she declared, "is fit only for the drain."

"In that case," my friend replied, "I must be an outsize drain because I think it is one of the best wines that can be had today."

So, you see, it is all a matter of taste. And what is more important is knowing in advance which wines you like, and so narrowing your choice to those that really matter.

## GINGER WINE

This is an alcoholic ginger wine of roughly the same strength as other home-made wines. The ginger and acids may be obtained from almost any chemist.

14 g (½ oz) ginger essence, 7 g (¼ oz) tartaric acid, 7 g (¼ oz) cream of tartar, 0.9 kg (2 lb) sugar, all-purpose wine yeast or dried yeast from a branch of *Heath and Heather*, nutrient and approximately 4.5 l (1 gallon) of water.

*Method for ginger wine*

Boil 4 l (7 pints) of water for 2 min and while boiling pour over the sugar in fermenting vessel. Allow to cool slightly and then mix in the two acids. Add 150 ml (0.25 pint) of freshly made tea and the yeast and ferment, covered as directed, in warm place for 5 days. Add nutrient, and pour carefully into 4.5 l (1 gallon) jar, leaving as much deposit behind as you can. There will be very little of this compared with the deposit left by fruit wines. If the jar is not filled to where neck begins, fill to this level with cooled boiled water. Fit fermentation lock and leave until all fermentation ceases. When this has happened, it will be found that the wine is dry, so sweeten to taste with saccharin. This is necessary because we have used only enough sugar to make a wine of slightly less than normal alcohol content. Adding more sugar would give rise to more fermentation and a wine too strong for its type. Add one sweetening tablet at a time and sample for sweetness, adding more if necessary. Bottle when clear and use as soon as you wish.

## POMEGRANATE WINE

I wonder how many older people remember the delight they used to obtain from pomegranates when they were children. Those orange-like fruits packed with a multitude of flesh-coloured pips make excellent wines, though I have not yet come upon a recipe elsewhere. Like most other fruit, they make three types of wines, though I prefer only two – dry and medium dry. If the pomegranates are not fully ripe when bought, keep them on a window-ledge that gets plenty of sunshine for about a week.

The following recipes may be used with the following method.

*For dry wine*

8 pomegranates, 1 kg (2.25 lb) sugar, all-purpose wine yeast, nutrient, tea as in method, 0.2 kg (0.5 lb) raisins, and approximately 4.5 l (1 gallon) of water.

*For medium sweet*

8 pomegranates, 1.1 kg (2.5 lb) sugar, all-purpose wine yeast, nutrient, tea as in method, 0.2 kg (0.5 lb) raisins and approximately 4.5 l (1 gallon) of water.

*For sweet*

10 pomegranates, 1.4 kg (3 lb) sugar, 0.2 kg (0.5 lb) raisins, tea as in method, all-purpose wine yeast, nutrient and approximately 4.5 l (1 gallon) of water.

*Method for pomegranate wines*

Skin the pomegranates, put the fleshy pips in fermenting vessel and crush by hand. Add raisins. Boil half the sugar to be used in 3.4 l (3 quarts) of water for 2 min and when cool pour over the crushed fruit. Add 150 ml (0.25 pint) freshly made tea, yeast and nutrient, and ferment in warm place, covered as directed, for 7 days. Strain out solids. Boil remaining sugar in 0.61 l (1 pint) of water for 2 min and when cool add to the mixture. Continue to ferment in fermentation vessel, covered as before, for 3 more days. Then pour carefully into 4.5 l (1 gallon) jar, leaving as much deposit behind as you can. If the jar is not filled to where neck begins, fill to this level with cooled boiled water. Fit fermentation lock and leave in warm place until all fermentation ceases. When this has happened, remove lock and bung, fit new bung as tightly as possible and put wine in cool place to clear. When clear, put half in a 2.25 l (0.5 gallon) jar and bottle remainder.

The dry and medium dry may be used while quite young, but the sweeter wine should kept for at least a year.

## PARSLEY WINE

This wine is gaining enormous popularity, not only because it is very cheap but because it makes a very excellent wine, especially when made dry for table use. As this is not a wine to make sweet, do not exceed the amounts of sugar in the recipes.

*For dry wine*

0.5 kg (1 lb) parsley, 1 kg (2.25 lb) sugar, 2 oranges, 2 lemons, tea as in method, all-purpose wine yeast, nutrient and approximately 4.5 l (1 gallon) of water.

*For medium dry*

0.5 kg (1 lb) parsley, 1.2 kg (2.75 lb) sugar, 2 oranges, 2 lemons, tea as in method, all-purpose wine yeast, nutrient and approximately 4.5 l (1 gallon) of water.

*Method for parsley wines*

Rinse parsley under fast running tap and shake free of water. Boil parsley in 4 l (7 pints) of water for 20 min and strain, while boiling, over *all* the sugar in fermenting vessel, stirring until all is dissolved. When cool, add cut up oranges and lemons and their peel. Add 150 ml (0.25 pint) of freshly made tea, yeast and nutrient, and ferment in warm place, covered as directed. After 5 days give the oranges and lemons a thorough squeezing and remove the peel. Continue to ferment in vessel for total of 8–10 days. Then strain; pour carefully into 4.5 l (1 gallon) jar, leaving as much deposit behind as you can. If the jar is not filled to where neck begins, fill to this level with cooled boiled water. Then fit fermentation lock and leave in warm place until all fermentation has ceased. When this has happened, remove lock and bung, fit new bung as tightly as possible and put wine in cool place to clear. When clear, put half in a 2.25 l (0.5 gallon) jar and bottle remainder.

Both these wines may be used quite young.

## CLOVE WINE

This is not a wine I like, but a lot of people do. Many swear that there is nothing better than to give this to your guests as they depart into the cold. In my view, the fact that it warms you up is all there is to commend it. But I must concede that it is popular with certain people, and as I have been careful to explain, the whole basis of successful wine-making lies in making the types which you personally like. So if you think you would like a wine flavoured with cloves, this recipe is just what you are looking for.

Any basic ingredient will do for this, but most people seem to go for those producing red wines. On no account use expensive or scarce ingredients because the flavour of cloves will obliterate their flavour and they will be wasted.

Before going on to the recipe, let me just say this: my mother, who experienced some really terrific failures on occasions, used to doctor her wine with cloves and regale visitors with the stuff. And I cannot recall any of them refusing a second glass. Naturally, I would not suggest that you stoop to such practices in the event of a great misfortune which results in your turning out a disappointing wine – but it's a trick worth remembering!

The ingredients are as follows:
1.4 kg (3 lb) beetroots, 0.2 kg (0.5 lb) packeted dates, 1.4 kg (3 lb) sugar, juice of 3 lemons, 150 ml (0.25 pint) of tea, 10 cloves, all-purpose wine yeast, nutrient and approximately 4.5 l (1 gallon) of water.

Do not peel the beetroots but scrub them thoroughly and then grate or slice them finely. Put them in 3.4 l (3 quarts) of water, bring to the boil and simmer for 15 min. Put half the sugar to be used in fermenting vessel with chopped dates and freshly made tea. Strain the beetroots, while boiling, over the sugar and dates, stirring until sugar is dissolved. Allow mixture to cool, add strained lemon juice, yeast and nutrient. Cover as advised and ferment for 10 days in warm place. Strain out dates, put strained wine into 4.5 l (1 gallon) jar and fit fermentation lock. Leave to ferment for further 7–8 days. Transfer wine to another jar, leaving as much deposit behind as you can. Boil remaining sugar in 0.6 l (1 pint) of water for 2 min and when cool add to the jar. This will not fill to where neck begins, so fill to this level with cooled boiled water. Then add cloves, fit fermentation lock and ferment in warm place until all fermentation ceases. Strain wine to remove cloves and put in cool place to clear, tightly bunged down. When clear, put half in a 2.25 l (0.5 gallon) jar and bottle remainder.

Some improvement does take place on keeping, but, generally, this wine may be used as soon as it is brilliant.

## PARSLEY AND PEA POD WINE

A surprisingly good wine is made from these cheap and simple ingredients. It is best to make two types of wines from these, rather than three. When sweet, it tends to lack flavour unless a large amount of ingredients are used, and then the flavour is spoiled. So make either medium sweet or dry.

*Dry wine*

0.5 kg (1 lb) fresh parsley, 0.5 kg (1 lb) pea pods (on no account allow peas in – not even one, however small), 0.5 kg (1 lb) sultanas, juice of 2 lemons, 150 ml (0.25 pint) freshly made strong tea, 0.9 kg (2 lb) sugar, yeast, nutrient and approximately 4.5 l (1 gallon) of water.

*Medium sweet wine*

0.5 kg (1 lb) fresh parsley, 0.5 kg (1 lb) pea pods (no peas – see recipe above), 0.7 kg (1.5 lb) raisins, juice of 2 lemons, 150 ml (0.25 pint) of freshly made tea, 1.1 kg (2.5 lb) sugar, yeast, nutrient and approximately 4.5 l (1 gallon) of water.

*Method for parsley and pea pod wines*

Wash parsley and pea pods and cut up fairly small. Put them in fermenting vessel with the chopped sultanas (or raisins, according to which recipe is being used) and add the tea. Boil half the sugar in 3.4 l (3 quarts) of water for 2 min and, while boiling, pour over the ingredients. Allow to cool and then add strained lemon juice, yeast and nutrient. Cover as directed and ferment in warm place for 5 days, stirring daily. Strain out solids and wring out fairly dry. Return strained wine to cleaned fermenting vessel. Boil remaining sugar in 0.6 l (1 pint) of water for 2 min and when cool add to the rest. Cover as before and continue to ferment for further 8–10 days. Then transfer to 4.5 l (1 gallon) jar, leaving as much deposit behind as you can. If this does not fill to where neck begins, fill to this level with cooled boiled water. Then fit fermentation lock and leave in warm place until all fermentation has ceased. When this has happened, remove lock and bung and fit new bung as tightly as possible and put wine in cool place to clear. When clear, put half in a 2.25 l (0.5 gallon) jar and bottle remainder.

The dry may be used quite young, but turns into a surprisingly delightful wine if kept for a year. The medium sweet should be kept for a year before use, and will be much better if kept longer.

## MALT WINE

Another surprisingly good wine. This may be made medium sweet or sweet, but it is not suitable to make dry.

*Sweet wine*

0.5 kg (1 lb) beetroot, 0.5 kg (1 lb) malt, 0.5 kg (1 lb) raisins, 1.4 kg (3 lb) sugar, juice of 2 lemons, 150 ml (0.25 pint) freshly made strong tea, yeast, nutrient and approximately 4.5 l (1 gallon) of water.

*Medium sweet wine*

Use the above ingredients but use only 1.3 kg (2.75 lb) sugar.

*Method for malt wines*

Do not peel beetroots but scrub them thoroughly and grate or slice finely. Put them in 2.3 l (2 quarts) of water and bring to boil and simmer gently for 15 min. Strain while boiling onto the raisins and malt in fermenting vessel. Boil half the sugar in 1.1 l (1 quart) of water for 2 min and pour onto the rest. Add tea. Allow to cool and add strained lemon juice, yeast and nutrient. Cover as advised and ferment in warm place for 8–10 days, stirring daily. Strain out solids and wring out fairly dry. Return strained wine to cleaned fermenting vessel. Boil remaining sugar in 0.6 l (1 pint) of water for 2 min and when cool add to the rest. Leave covered as before to ferment in warm place for further 5–6 days.

Transfer to 4.5 l (1 gallon) jar, leaving as much deposit behind as you can. Then, if this does not fill to where neck of jar begins, fill to this level with cooled boiled water. Fit fermentation lock and leave in warm place until all fermentation has ceased. When this has happened remove lock and bung, fit new bung as tightly as possible and put wine in cool place to clear. When clear, put half in a 2.25 l (0.5 gallon) jar and bottle remainder.

Both these wines improve a great deal with age, so I do hope you will keep some for a least two years.

*Chapter Ten*

# SOME QUESTIONS AND ANSWERS

There are inevitably one or two points which cannot be covered in a book of this sort. The recipes are straightforward enough, the methods too, for that matter. But it must be borne in mind that my methods and the directions in other parts of this book are general purpose instructions, to be carried out under normal conditions. If everything goes according to plan, questions are hardly likely to arise, but on occasion, everything does not go according to plan. I suppose it is a case of "the best laid schemes of mice and men". So, just in case something goes wrong, let me try to answer your questions before you have need to ask them. The questions are a cross-section of those I receive from all over the world.

*Feeding with raisins*

Q. I have a collection of rather old recipes that advise adding a couple of raisins to each bottle of wine which must be left with the cork "popped in" loosely for at least six weeks. Then I am to cork hard and put the wine in a cool place to clear. I have been following these directions, and although some wines have not been too bad, hardly any have come up to expectations. Some have taken on a strong taste of vinegar.

The idea of adding the raisins, according to the recipe, is to feed the yeast and therefore make a better wine. But it does not seem to work out. Would you please tell me what you think of these recipes and of the idea of feeding with raisins.

A. My advice to you is to burn the recipes and forget that you have ever read them, let alone used them. Then start wine-making afresh using modern methods and recipes.

I say this because it is obvious that these recipes come from an era when hardly anybody knew the first thing about wine-making, and when no one knew the difference between a good home-made wine and a poor one. If this were not true, the recipe would not have advised "popping the cork in loosely for weeks". This is, or was, the main cause of wine turning to vinegar, and for making it disappointing in other ways. It is obvious then that the recipes were evolved long ago when practically nothing was known about the subject.

*Fusal oil in potatoes*

Q. I have been making wines for some time now using the methods and recipes in your book *Successful Modern Wine-Making*, and I have been most successful. Now a friend tells me that potatoes produce fusal oil so that all my potato wines are dangerous. I have several sorts, some made with raisins, some with sultanas, and so on, and all are really good wines.

A. It is perfectly true that potatoes produce fusal oil in wine, and when people tell others this it is usually to let them think they know a great deal about the subject. They obviously do not, otherwise they would also know that the amount of fusal oil produced is so infinitesimal, and is diluted to such an extent, that it is rendered quite harmless. So drink up and enjoy them.

*So little fruit*

Q. What puzzles me about making wines from wild and garden fruit is that when we use these we use just a few pounds, but when using grapes we use all grapes and no water. Why can't we do this with wild and garden fruits?

Surely we would get much better wine – that is, stronger flavours, more bouquet, aroma and alcohol?

A. Fact is, you would get nothing of the sort. In fact, the wine would have such an overpowering flavour and bouquet and aroma – not to mention an acidity that would make you screw your face into a pantomime mask – that the wine would be quite unpalatable.

Grapes – as I have mentioned elsewhere – are the ideal medium for making wines because they usually contain all the necessary elements for a good wine in the right proportions. But English fruits do not. Therefore we have to dilute in order to reduce the strength of flavour and the acid content. Hence the abundance of recipes calling for amounts usually between 1.4 and 2.3 kg (3 and 5 lb) of English fruits.

*"Rope" in wine*

Q. This is not a trouble I have had in recent years because I have been following modern methods, but years ago I made some orange wine that was excellent when I put it away in store. But when I went to use it, it had developed an overpowering flavour and bouquet, with a certain amount of acidity that was not there when I put it in store. When I poured it down the sink, what looked like a short coil of rope came out of the jar. I know there was nothing like this in the jar when I put the wine into it. Would you please tell me what happened?

A. It is a good job you poured that wine down the sink, because even modern remedies usually turn out to be a waste of time in cases like this.

This trouble is caused by lactic acid bacteria. Modern methods prevent this trouble, so you are not likely to have it again. Oh, you are quite right, that piece of rope was not in the jar when you put the wine in. First of all, the wine, when affected in this manner, takes on an oily appearance, and then threads appear in it. Only after a long time does that coil of "rope" form.

*Renewed fermentation*

Q. I make wines as soon as cherries are available, and continue throughout the summer until the last of the fruits are about. What puzzles me is that those made early in the year ferment properly and never give trouble later on. But blackberry, elderberry and damson wines – my three favourites – always seem to give trouble.

Fermentation goes on perfectly from start to finish and I then put them away. They are always beautifully clear and ready for drinking. But I like to keep them because I know from experience how much they improve. But round about February there are several loud "pops" from under the stairs where I store my wines, and I find that these three wines are fermenting again. Why should some react in this fashion and others not?

A. These are three of my favourites, too, and I make them regularly.

You will notice that these three wines are made late in summer. This means that fermentation is still going on when the cold weather comes. And it is upon a cold night in late autumn or early winter that the yeast stops fermenting because the wine has become cold. Later, when a warm spell turns up – usually in February or, perhaps, a little later – warmth penetrates to the wine and the yeast becomes active again. Although this is a nuisance, you will get a far better wine in the end.

Put the wine into a jar, fit fermentation lock and leave in a warm place until all fermentation has ceased again. To prevent this trouble try to keep the wine in a warm place throughout fermentation – even when the nights turn cold. The reason this does not happen with wines made early in the year is because of warm weather throughout the fermentation period.

*Too sweet*

Q. I have some blackberry wine that is much too sweet. I must have accidentally used too much sugar because I know that the alcohol content is high. By this I mean that I know fermentation went on long enough to use up sufficient sugar to leave a medium dry wine which I prefer. Therefore, I must have used too much sugar. Can you tell me how to reduce the sugar content?

A. If you mean remove some of the sugar, I am afraid I cannot help you. But if you have a very dry wine of similar nature to the blackberry – say blackcurrant or elderberry – then it would be a good plan to blend the very dry with the sweet until you get the blackberry to your liking. On the other hand, if you do not want to blend, you will have to wait until next season and then make plenty of blackberry wine bone dry by using 200g of sugar to the litre (2 lb sugar per gallon) and no dried fruit. When this is finished, you may blend the two wines to your liking. But let me add that it often takes much more of the dry to reduce the sweetness. Therefore, if you have 4.5 l (1 gallon) of the over-sweet, make 9 l (2 gallons) of very dry. In this way you will have enough dry wine to reduce the sweetness of the other quite effectively.

*Too dry*

Q. I thought I liked dry wines until I made some using 200g of sugar to the litre (2 lb sugar per gallon). Now I find that it must be medium dry to medium sweet wines that I like. Would you please tell me what to do to sweeten these.

A. First of all, you can do the exact opposite to my reply to the query "too sweet" above, or you may sweeten these over-dry wines with ordinary sugar.

If you choose the latter method, take about 0.6 l (1 pint) from 4.5 l (1 gallon) and put this in a china or polythene jug, stand the jug in a saucepan of water over heat and add a teaspoonful of sugar for each bottle – six bottles for each 4.5 l (1 gallon). Warm the wine in this manner, stirring to dissolve the sugar. When all is dissolved, allow this to cool and mix in well with the bulk. Sample this, and if it is sweet enough, all well and good. If not, repeat the process, but please do go carefully with the next lot of sugar, as it is very easy to over-sweeten.

Your query pin-points one of the major problems of wine-making – deciding in advance whether you like wines dry, medium or otherwise. And it is only by experience of this sort that most people find out where their preferences lie.

*Fermentation lock puzzle*

Q. I am using the recipe in your excellent book *Successful Modern Wine-making,* and what puzzles me is that with one batch of wine the fermentation lock seems to have gone haywire. First, bubbles pass through quite normally, then, next day, bubbles are passing the opposite way, meaning that air is being drawn into the jar. I am not over-worried about this, as the sterilizing solution in the lock will purify the air. What really puzzles me is what is causing this to happen.

A. Obviously, your wine is in a place where it is warm one minute and cold the next. This is evident by the fact that bubbles pass through as they should and then go the opposite way. This is caused by the wine becoming cold so that it contracts – shrinks. This causes space to be left in the jar so that air must be drawn in to make it up. When the wine becomes warm again, the wine expands and compresses the air in the jar so that bubbles pass through in the normal way. If you keep your wine in a fairly constant temperature throughout fermentation you will not experience this again.

*Acid wine*

Q. I have 9 l (2 gallons) of wine that has turned out rather "sharp", or "tart", as I have heard it called, but I suppose it boils down to the fact that it is over-acid. The wine is really good apart from this, and there is certainly no evidence that it might have gone wrong. Is it possible to reduce this acidity without reducing the flavour of the wine?

A. This depends on the type of wine. If it is rhubarb, taking out the acid will certainly alter the flavour. This is because nearly all the flavour in this wine comes from the oxalic acid present. So, if you remove the acid, you will also remove the flavour. But if it is any other wine, the acidity probably comes from using under-ripe fruits which contain much too much acid.

The remedy for this is to blend it with a similar wine that lacks acid. Or make a similar wine low in acid for the purpose of blending with the acid wine. Alternatively, use precipitated chalk from a chemist and work as follows. The chalk costs about 1p per 25g (1p per oz).

Take 1.1 l (1 quart) of the wine, and from this take about a cupful; into this cupful stir a teaspoonful of the chalk, and then stir this into the remaining 1.1 l (1 quart). Leave this to become brilliant again and then siphon the clear wine off the chalk deposit. The treated quart will contain no acid because the chalk will have crystallized it so that it has settled to the bottom with the chalk. Put the treated wine with the rest of the gallon, and the overall effect will be that you have reduced the acid in 4.5 l (1 gallon) by a quarter. If it is still too "sharp" repeat the process. Be careful not to take out too much acid otherwise you will have to add some to rectify matters. If you do happen to take out too much, take a little of the wine and dissolve a few crystals of citric acid from a chemist in this, and then stir into the bulk. Repeat if necessary. Citric acid costs about 2½p per 25g (2½p per oz).

*How much yeast?*

Q. I have made wines by what you would call "granny's method", using baker's yeast, and I always used about 25 g per litre (1 oz per gallon). But I am using wine yeast now with more modern methods and am puzzled by directions supplied with the yeast. These say one tablet for up to 22.5 l (5 gallons), while another supplier says one tablet for up to 13.5 l (3 gallons). What puzzles me is whether the amount of yeast added makes any difference to the wine.

A. The amount of yeast added does not make a scrap of difference to the finished wine, but it makes a great deal of difference to the rate of fermentation. For example, if you add a pin-head of yeast it will start to ferment very slowly, but as the yeast reproduces itself there will quickly become more and more yeast to increase the rate of fermentation. This is why when you add a little yeast you end up with, at least, a 12.5 mm (0.5 in) layer of it in the jar or fermentation vessel. When you transfer to a jar, leaving as much deposit behind as you can, you do this to prevent too much yeast and fruit waste coming over into the jar as well. But in a few weeks, you will have another layer of yeast in the jar. This is because it continues to reproduce itself. So you can, in effect, add as little or as much yeast as you like. If you add too much, you may find fermentation so vigorous that the polythene cover is blown up like a balloon and the wine froths over the side of the vessel. Or, as one chap writing to me put it: "the darn stuff all but chased me round the kitchen".

Yeast tablets are in a convenient form and one to each 4.5 l (1 gallon) is usually enough, but you can add two to each 4.5 l (1 gallon) if you want to.

*Bread crock*

Q. I have an old bread crock – at least I am told that this is what it is – that my mother used to make wines in. The glaze looks to be in perfect condition, but I have been told that this could be lead-glazed, and in this event it might give lead into the wine and, subsequently, give me lead poisoning if I drink my wines. Well, I want to drink my wines, so could you please tell me whether this crock is safe to use or not?

A. Without seeing this crock I doubt whether I could tell you whether it is safe to use or not. And even if I did see it, I might not be able to tell, because it needs an expert to distinguish the different types of glaze used.

Your best plan is not to use it, thus avoiding the risk; after all, a good polythene pail costs less than 32½p and certainly, a lot less than a dose of lead poisoning.

*Screw to bottles*

Q. I store large amounts of wines in bottles for several years before using, and it occurs to me that the best way would be to use screw-top bottles, provided the rubber bands are in good condition. But before I go over to these I would appreciate your opinion.

A. A good many years ago I came in for a good deal of criticism for recommending screw-top bottles. I had overlooked the fact that I was writing for beginners who would not be able to tell for sure whether fermentation had ceased for good. If wine is put into screw-top bottles and fermentation recommences – and we have seen that it can and often does – the gas cannot blow out the stopper as it can a cork. The result would be that, if fermentation happened to go on long enough, all those bottles would become as dangerous as hand-grenades with the pins pulled.

Bear in mind that yeast can live and ferment without air, so cutting off the air supply makes no difference if more fermentation wanted to take place. And I am quite serious about the hand-grenade description. The gas would become so compressed that, in the end, the bottle would go off like a bomb.

*Selling wine*

Q. I have some really marvellous wines and have been asked to sell a few bottles to friends at Christmas. Am I allowed by law to do this?

A. No.

*Storage problem*

Q. The only problem I have in this fascinating business is that of storage. I have over 225 l (50 gallons) and as I add a 10 l or so (about 2 gallons) to the store so I take the same quantity and bottle it. This bottled stuff I keep under the stairs, not only because it is a convenient place to store in, but also because it is a convenient place to reach.

But what bothers me is the bulk wines in jars. The only place I have for storing these is an outhouse that remains fairly cool during hot weather, but becomes intensely cold in winter. Water freezes in this outhouse. Is it safe to keep wines in this?

A. Certainly. I hope that your outhouse keeps cool in summer, which is most important. The fact that it gets frozen out in winter does not matter. The alcohol in the wine will prevent the wine freezing – so there is no risk of burst jars, and no harm is likely to occur to the wine owing to cold.

# APPENDIX

The following is a list of the firms supplying special ingredients, utensils and all other requirements.

Semplex, Old Hall Works, Stuart Road, Higher Tranmere, Birkenhead, Cheshire.

W. R. Loftus, 24 Tottenham Court Road, London, W.1.

Joseph Bryant Limited, 95 Old Market Street, Bristol, 2.

Winemaker Equipment Limited, 242 Deansgate, Manchester, 3.

Home Winemakers Supplies, 28 Swan Street, Manchester, 4.

Leigh-Williams and Sons, 9 Easter Drive, Grassendale, Liverpool, 19.

Brew It Yourself, 208–209 Upper Street, Islington, London, N.1.

Handicrafts and Utilities Limited, 42–43 Mary Street, Southampton.

W. A. Revitt and Company, Ashforth Street, Nottingham.

Hoyle's Home Wine-making Supplies, 131–133 Main Street, Auchinlek, Ayrshire: sole distributors in Scotland.

*In Canada*
Wine Art, P.O. Box 2701, Vancouver 3, B.C. (Also serves large areas of U.S.A.)

*In U.S.A.*
Aetne Bottle Company Inc., 708 Rainer Avenue South, Seattle 44, Washington.

*In New Zealand*
Brewers Trading Company, P.O. Box 593, Christchurch.